# Tribal Skills and Philosophies in Times of Crisis

# Tribal Skills and Philosophies in Times of Crisis

**Dr Longshibeni N Kithan**

KALPAZ

*Published by*

Kalpaz Publications
C-30, Satyawati Nagar,
Delhi – 110052
Ph.: 011-47034999, 9811692060
www.kalpazpublications.com
E-mail: kalpaz@hotmail.com

*Distribution Network*
gyanbooks.com
India, USA, Canada, UK, Australia, France



ISBN: 978-93-5722-287-7

First Published, 2023

*Printed at:* Gyan Press, Delhi.



**TRIBAL SKILLS AND PHILOSOPHIES IN TIMES OF CRISIS**

Author: DR LONGSHIBENI N KITHAN

# Contents

# Preface

The heterogeneity of tribes and their problems in India have opened avenues for many new debates and deliberations. To a greater extent, the rapidly transitioning Indian Tribes have made it complex to theorise and even universalise the concept of tribes and their problems. Constitutionally recognised as Scheduled Tribes, though, they encompass 8.6 percent of the Indian population, comprising 705 (2011 census) throughout the length and breadth of India. Despite 76 years of Independence, many tribes, particularly in remote rural areas, continue to be exploited for the natural resources viz. Land, water, forest, and minerals. In addition, displacement and indebtedness, increasing vulnerability of their language, culture, and identity, poverty, poor health, and education infrastructure, including decent roads, water, and sanitation are ongoing problems.

The process of assimilation of many tribes other than the tribes of most parts of Northeast India has led to a significant loss of cultural identity. Furthermore, some state-initiated development paradigms have not addressed this but instead reinforced it through the majoritarian stance, resulting in further alienation of tribes. The state-sponsored development paradigm and the interest of the corporations preceded the voice of the tribes too. Consequently, increased militarisation by imposing alarming troops, BSFs, and police personnel have not only terrorised most parts of Northeast India and central India but severed the already sore relationship, which continues to be largely unaddressed. In view of this, the emergence of newer problems of climate change, environmental destruction, global hunger, exploitative market forces etc., would be detrimental to the already vulnerable position of the tribals. Significantly, although several commissions and committees were formed over the decades with the supposed state commitment to address the emerging tribal problems, the desired outcome has not been achieved. As a result, scholars have argued that the development paradigm needs to be more holistic and realistic.

However, what can be seen as a ray of hope is that there has been increasing global recognition of tribal philosophies and skills potentials.

Scholars have argued that Tribals in India have, for a long time, developed skills and philosophies in close association with the local environment that enabled healthy human, beyond human, and more than human interaction. This recognition of tribes is often perceived as distinct from most non-tribal societies today. The present discussions in the book also suggest a symbiotic relationship between humans and non-human counterparts such as plants, animals, and natural resources like forests, land, and water to be not exploitative but sustainable. Furthermore, despite the unprecedented changes in the tribal landscape, both natural and human, made prior to independence and post-independence, their cultural adaptation process has shown increasing resiliencies.

It is also significant to mention that; the oral tradition has been an integral part of most Tribal ways of life for enabling the effective transmission of knowledge from one generation to the other. In the face of modernity, though, there have been challenges to facilitating the traditional transmission mode of knowledge, particularly with the present young generation. Most of this knowledge is confined to the elderly, soon-dying generation and there is an urgent need to bridge the intergenerational gap.

Given this, this collaborative effort provides significant insights, though by no means covers every issue relevant to numerous Indian tribes. The present work is a modest attempt to serve as a repository of the dying cultural heritage of some Indian tribes and bring to the fore the tribal experiences, opinions, aspirations, and priorities with the hope of contributing a minuscule role to the above inadequacies.

Although the current edited book mostly includes the selected papers presented in each technical session, the participation of the Invited Speakers is acknowledged and briefly summarised here:

Prof. Bengt G Karlsson (Stokholm University, Sweden) delivered the keynote address and other invited speakers include Dr. Sophie Chao (University of Sydney, Australia), Jelle J P Wouters (Royal Thimpu college, Bhutan), Virginius Xaxa (IIHD, New Delhi), Prof. Chellaperumal (Pondicherry University, India), Leishipem Khamrang (Royal Thimpu college, Bhutan). The Conference also witnesssed participation of experts in thematic sessions viz., Prof. Lucy Zehol, Prof. Ajailiu Newmai, Dr. Rocky Raile Zipao, Dr. Kanato Chophi, Amba Jamir, Prof. Channaveer RM, Prof. Simon John, Dr. Archana Kujur, and Dr. Lakshmana G.

**Lucy Zehol** raises the question of reviving Indigenous/traditional institutions with a notion of ecological stability and social harmony in the

Naga context. She approaches the Human and Natural resources through a gender lens, considering the diversity in Naga culture. She looks at how gender roles impact inequalities towards women in three aspects contributing to natural abuse. She also discusses the challenges critiquing the notion of eco-feminist that exacerbate gender inequalities and recommends transforming formal structures.

**Longshibeni Kithan** discusses the historical process of decentralisation and its effectiveness in addressing contemporary issues surrounding domestic water supply in Yikhum village of Wokha district. She argued that, the Decentralisation has strengthened Lotha's traditional principles, and values, and resulted in improved delivery of water but the issue of women underrepresentation in important water decisions remain unaddressed. Therefore, the author suggests more nuanced analyses of traditional norms of men in decision making.

**Khajungla Tangvah** discusses the indigenous technologies and knowledge used by the farmers in rice cultivation with special emphasis on jhum and terrace cultivations of Khambi and Nungbi Khullen village of Ukhrul district, Manipur. She notes indigenous knowledge as the ground of decision policy making for sustainable development (food security), particularly women as the agent of indigenous knowledge. Therefore, Innovation in traditional knowledge systems must be encouraged so that individuals can find new opportunities to mitigate the effects of the scarcity of natural resources, drought, and unfavourable market conditions.

**Visakhono and Kanato** discuss entomophagy in Nagaland as a sustainable practice and an age-old knowledge system that is rooted in cultural beliefs and economic livelihood of the people. Taking the case of locusts as a food source, the chapter explores the relationship between agricultural practices, traditional knowledge systems and sustainable practices in the light of food security and climate change facing the Naga communities of Nagaland.

**Clarissa** discusses the Ñiam Tre religious philosophies around nature and environment of the people of Nangbah through the various religious rites performed; tries to delineate the extent and impact of modernity and globalisation on traditional practices and discusses a need for environmental awareness among the people with regard to sustainability in their ritual practices through a structure based functional approach and a symbolic-interaction approach. With the rise of modernisation, development should be realised from the cultural ethics and it should come from the people.

**Hemant Tigga and Neishoning Koireng** explore the spiritual life and worldview of Oraons through a literature review. It seeks the lessons of sustainability to the global problem in the cultural actions of Oraons to, which is intrinsically rooted in their spirituality. He concludes his argument that spirituality increases people's awareness and observance of their inner and outer worlds in general. It makes a significant contribution toward modifying what is required. Furthermore, Spiritual people are more sensitive and eager to make significant and constructive changes to see the environment as a reflection of them, and spirituality is inextricably related to humanity.

**Mhasileno Peseyie and Rashmi Gaur** provide insight into the folk narratives in protecting the community's sacred environment and the applicability of integrated indigenous traditional knowledge. Some selective Naga Folktales are analyzed through the theoretical framework of folk narratives and interpretive content analysis. These folk narratives reflect both the individual and the community. The folktales employ the indigenous knowledge as a guide and establish the moral messages, including conserving their environment, which is delivered through the characters and practices, either explicitly or implicitly. This paper suggest that Naga folktales embedded with environment-related themes in promoting indigenous knowledge, which can play a vital role in adaptation effort and climate change assessment.

**Tame Ramya**, In the article, "Indigenous Knowledge in Natural Resource Management: An Observation of the Practices among Nyishi Tribe of Arunachal Pradesh," surveys the significance of Indigenous knowledge (IK) practiced by the Nyishi tribe in Arunachal Pradesh, India. Primarily, he discusses the varied use of indigenous knowledge by the Nyishi tribe in all aspects of their life. She observes the widely used plants for medicinal purposes within the community. He further suggests documenting the significant indigenous knowledge practiced by the tribal people.

**Shima Saha** proposes a different story where the local knowledge in healing practices is not only considered as stimuli among the tea tribes of the Alipurduar district of West Bengal but also encounters the way the modern health system is operationalised. These practices can act as a model for sustainable development in adaptation to changing ecology.

**Ketousieno Kuotsuo** discusses the ethnomedicine/traditional medicine that plays a crucial role among the Angami Nagas of Viphoma Village. In her findings, this particular community benefits enormously from medicinal plants, animal products, ethno medical specialists and faith healers. Despite modern healthcare, practicing traditional healing methods as an alternative and complementary medical system in an age where modern medicine has dominated the system of diagnosing and treating illness is suggested.

**Lunminthang Lhouvam** discusses how the various beliefs and practices of the Thadou of Manipur aid in the management and maintenance of their natural surroundings. The close proximity and intimate relationship shared between them help them co-exist successfully as a part of the ecological system.

**Abhishek Kumar and Amit Kumar** discuss the use of indigenous medicinal practices by the Korku Tribe of Melghat, Yavatmal region. Due to lack of proper medical facilities, Korku rely on the traditional medicinal practices. The study suggests to promote the traditional medicinal practices to increase the efficacy of healing the ailments and illnesses.

**Jenny Jami** discusses the issues surrounding local perception and adaptability to newer learning and learning aids among learners in higher education in Nagaland during Corona Pandemic.

# Acknowledgement

The present Volume is mostly a collection of selected papers presented at the International Conference on "Indigenous Knowledge and Climate Change: Issue, Challenges and Coping mechanisms", between 25th to 27th October 2022. It also includes few papers from scholars in the field of Tribal research.

The review process was herculean and it would not have taken place effectively without the patience, and cooperation from the paper contributors. I owe my gratitude to all. I also extend my gratitude to my family members and friends for the patience and understanding while conceptualising this Project.

Last but not the least, I want to thank the Department colleagues for their encouragement, and the Kalpaz Publications for the willingness to publish the Book.

**Longshibeni N Kithan**

# About the Contributors

**Dr Lucy Zehol** is a Professor of Anthropology and Dean of the School of Human and Envronmental Sciences, North Eastern Hill University.

**Dr Longshibeni N Kithan** is an Assistant Professor of Socio-cultural Anthropology at the Department of Folkloristics and Tribal studies, Central University of Karnataka.

**Dr Khajungla Tangvah** is an Independent researcher based in Shillong, Meghalaya.

**Dr Visakhonu Hibo** is the Principal of Japfu Christian College, Kohima, Nagaland.

**Dr G Kanato Chophy** is an Assistant Professor at the Department of Anthropology, Dibrugarh University, Assam.

**Dr Tame Ramya** is a researcher affiliated to the Department of Tribal Studies, Rajiv Gandhi University, Arunachal Pradesh.

**Ms Clarissa Candace Giri** is a Ph.D. candidate of the Department of Anthropology, North Eastern Hill University, Shillong, Meghalaya.

**Mr Hemant Tigga** is a Ph.D. candidate of the Department of Tribal Studies, Central University of Jharkhand, Jharkhand.

**Dr T. Neishoning Koireng** is an Assistant Professor at the Department of Tribal Studies, Central University of Jharkhand, Jharkhand.

**Ms Mhasileno Peseyie** is a Ph.D. candidate of the Department of Humanities and Social Sciences, Indian Institute of Technology Roorkee, Uttarakhand.

**Dr Rashmi Gaur** is a Professor at the Department of Humanities and Social Sciences, Indian Institute of Technology Roorkee, Uttarakhand.

**Mr Lunminthang Lhouvum** is a Ph.D. candidate of the Department of History, North Eastern Hill University, Meghalaya.

**Ms Shima Saha** is a Ph.D. candidate of the Department of Tribal Studies, Central University of Jharkhand, Jharkhand.

**Dr Ketousieno Kuotsuo** is an Assistant Professor at the Christ College, Meghalaya.

**Mr Abhishek Kumar** is a Ph.D. candidate of the Department of Tribal Studies, Central University of Jharkhand, Jharkhand.

**Mr Amit Kumar** is a Ph.D. candidate of the Department of Tribal Studies, Central University of Jharkhand, Jharkhand.

**Dr Jenny Jami** is an Assistant Professor at the Department of Anthropology, Saint Claret College, Ziro, Arunachal Pradesh.

# 1

# Mapping Gender and Natural Resource Dynamics in Naga Society

**Lucy Zehol**

## Abstract

This paper approaches the Human and Natural Resource dynamics in Naga society through the gender lens. She questions the notion of reviving Indigenous/traditional institutions on the assumption that the past constituted a period of ecological stability and social harmony using the political ecology theoretical framework to critique the eco-feminist perspective in the context of Nagas.

## Introduction

### I

In everyday conversation, however, the term 'gender' may more often be used interchangeably with 'sex' as a categorical reference, i.e., 'male' and 'female', two examples of 'gender'. The distinction between 'sex and gender' as analytical categories can be traced back to developments in sociological, medical sciences, and (social or cultural) anthropology of the twentieth century. Whereas Simone de Beauvoir's (1949) political criticism of the subordination of women, titled 'the second sex', linked the cultural devaluation of women in western society to biological differences between men and women. Gayle Rubin (1975) explored the notion of a sex or gender system whereby the 'raw resources' of male and female bodies become 'gendered' products through processes of socialisation, normative behaviours, hegemonic representation, etc.

The 'raw resources' referred to by Rubin were defined by a conception of biomedical differences between 'male' and 'female'. Research on chromosomes, gonads, differences between the genitals, hormones, brain size, anatomical structure (men have more grey matter, women have white matter), and secondary characteristics such as body fat distribution (including breasts) and body hair. Bio-medical research has consistently sought to link such differences to innate 'personalities or psychological explanations for perceived differences in behaviour and effective experiences, whereas sociologists and socio-cultural anthropologists, as well as many psychologists, have tended instead to focus on how symbolic meaning and practices are associated with biological features of 'sex' to 'cultural construct of gender'.

Since the1990s, theorists have drawn attention to the medical assignment of 'sex' at birth as a culturally constructed practice. Ruth Hubbard (1990) cites Anne Fausto-Sterling's estimation that 1- 2 percent of babies are born with ambiguous sexual characteristics (chromosomal, gonad, and genital sex does not always corroborate with one another) and proposes the existence of at least five sexes. Like Judith Butler, Hubbard sees the surgical procedures to 'correct' the genitals of intersex infants as an example of science being used to force 'natural' bodies to conform to cultural perceptions.

In response to the increasing abstraction of gender theory, with everything being reduced to cultural constructions, Toril Moi's essay 'what is a woman' (2001) argues the need to abandon the 'gender' concept altogether and return to a theory embedded within a material world. Her 'lived body' concept proposes that a person's identity interaction with experience of their world is directly related to the materiality of his/her body, its physical attributes and capacities, the reactions it evokes from others, and its 'situation' within a historically specific cultural environment. Moreover, the body's inhabitant has projects and goals that determine how a person interacts with this 'situation'. Thus, the limits of the 'gender concept' tend to imply that people are subject to the roles imposed upon them by 'culture' and transcended by the 'lived body' theory. The advantage of the 'lived body' conceptualisation is that it accommodates a dynamic aspect of gender on the individual level that can be generalised to the community members within an overall historical framework. However, as Young (2005) points out in the essay 'lived body versus gender', such a conceptualisation is more useful to describe the individual experience than macro-logical social structure and organisation. Young concludes that 'gender' continues to be necessary for political and sociological approaches to gender relations.

## II

In this paper, we shall look at the Human-Natural resource relations that concentrate mainly on the local context and the internal society (gender) dynamics as the drivers of ecological change by applying a political ecology framework to understanding the dynamics of resource management in the context of Nagaland. Peluso and Watts provide tools for thinking about conflicts and struggles engendered by the forms of access to, and control over resources. Moreover, its attentiveness to power relations inherent in defining, controlling, and managing nature suggests an alternative viewing of the link between environment and political action. (Peluso and Watts 2001:24-25).

Each Naga culture is distinct concerning its customs, traditions, languages, foods, dress, style, ethos etc. This distinctiveness further extends to the village level with each village differing in one way or another, as anthropologists such as Mary Douglas expressed it, "consonant with its culture and society as well. Each culture has a style, an ethos." Given such diversity, exceptions to the generalisations made in this paper are inevitable. Fortunately, Anthropology does not emphasize the local for its own sake; as Stanley Tambiah wrote, the point of ethnography is "to use the particular to say something about the general". (1970.1)

## III. Gender and Natural Resource Dynamics Land and Forest

We begin by mapping the relationship of Naga Women, and Naga Men to land and forest as these are the life support systems around which the Naga economy and the indigenous knowledge system evolve.

Land is one of Nagaland's most essential and productive natural resources. One can invest in this natural capital for a productive activity to generate wealth. In the present age of globalisation, this natural capital is moveable and can be converted into economic goods, e.g., used as a mortgage to secure loans. This natural capital can also be privatized, and ownership changed. Men can inherit the land, the most important and productive wealth for the Naga. However, it does not apply to their women. Naga society is a patrilineal system in which descent is traced through the paternal line. Men can inherit land and property, while women are granted only user rights. The (eldest) son inherits the ancestral property, whereas a daughter has no right to inherit the immovable property from her father or claim the ancestral property. Out of love and affection, she can be given a share of the father's property as a gift. However, such gift declaration should be made in the presence of kinsmen and in-laws as witnesses. A woman is entitled to use the gifted plot of land as long as she lives, and she has to return it to her brothers after her death. In some villages, women can transfer the gifted property to their daughter for one or two generations, after which they must return it to the brothers. In the absence of brothers, the land goes back to the clan. A widow can look after her family property as long as she remains under her deceased husband's roof.

According to customary laws, women in Naga societies cannot usually claim the children after divorce. Maintenance of an infant is given to the mother in case of divorce for a short period, which varies from village to village. Moreover, women are not allowed to participate in the Village Development Board and share their ideas regarding village administration. Women are excluded from participating in all critical decision-making institutions (Zehol, 2009). Therefore, Naga women's access to land resources and user rights are mediated by the Naga customary laws. Control rights are often subjected to Naga customary laws, which are one-sided and biased. The principles relating to the relationship between men and women show that rules were more favourable for men as husbands than women as wives, mainly where the inheritance of properties was concerned. In the customary law of the village, as in the other Naga villages like Khezhakeno, women had no equal rights with men in the political or administrative sphere though their role was seen to be essential for the proper functioning of the society. The recognition of Naga customary laws in Article 371A of the Constitution of India further marginalises women.

Women's lack of land ownership, especially immovable property, affect economic well-being, social status, political voices, and the risk of domestic violence. Above all, due to their low representation in decision-making forums, they have little say in the rules governing natural resource management now being a frame that shows participatory exclusion in environmental governance (NSHDR, 2004).

Forest is a storehouse of resources of various kinds like fuel wood, which is an integral part of a Naga kitchen, medicinal herbs, and raw materials needed for subsistence farming (green manure, fodder for cattle, etc.). Through their role, the forest also contributes to rural livelihoods by replenishing groundwater supplies and preventing soil erosion.

The forest has traditionally been and still is a source of a wide variety of wild plants, insects, and animals for the Naga people. Apart from wild animals and plants, many other Non-Timber Forest Products are commonly collected from the wild. Among these are medicinal plants, fruits, and roots; bamboo and cane materials used in basketry and handicraft industry, wax and wood oils such as pinewood, traditionally used for lightening purposes; broom grass and bamboo shoots, widely used in Naga cuisine. Government schemes under the approval of the Ministry of Environment and Forests in some villages regulate the extraction of timber and non-timber forest products. The rich mineral resources of the State have yet to be exploited; among these are petroleum and natural gas, marble, coal, and limestone (NSHDR, 2004).

Women and children are the main collectors of wild edible plants. On the other hand, men are traditionally involved in hunting in the spring, winter, and autumn seasons. Although hunting is still practiced to some extent, many animals like foxes, squirrels, deer, bears, wild boars, and monkeys have drastically decreased, and some species have disappeared. For example, The Hornbill is among the most endangered species in the North East region, owing to the loss of its habitat and rampant slaughtering for its meat, beak, and feathers. The Hornbill is a majestic bird held with great esteem, especially the Great Hornbill, the largest true Hornbill, whose tail feathers are used by most Naga tribes for traditional purposes, particularly on headgear. The Great Hornbill has earned itself a place in Naga culture. Hornbills also play a vital role in maintaining a healthy forest by dispersing plant seeds as they move about.

Sadly, the developmental and urbanisation activity has destroyed the natural environment where local animal and plant species have disappeared from the face of Nagaland during the past few decades alone. Due to intensive timber extraction activities in the 1980s, vast virgin forests were denuded. Felling of trees is now regulated, wherein timber and other forest products can be extracted only through working schemes and as per the Tree Farm Rules, 2002. The conservation initiatives of the State Government, village council, and local people, combined with the ban on hunting, timber extraction, and forest burning, led to an increase in the overall vegetation cover and regeneration of species at all levels, as per government reports. However, the question remains: how far is this true? (NSHDR, 2004).

Therefore, there is a gradual erosion of knowledge of local plants and species as the forests and commons, the basis of this knowledge, disappear. While rural Naga women are not the sole repositories of this knowledge, they are often the significant bearers of information on particular items, such as food-related forest produce. Also, while women have no direct role or say in community forest management, effective forest resource management, and its wise utilisation will provide both men and women with ecological benefits, life support systems, and resources.

## IV. Gender Roles and Relations

The gender division of labour is the basis for women's double work burden. Women's double burden of productive and reproductive work has been widely documented. Changing this is the most difficult, but women who are economically independent and have a political voice are also in a better position to negotiate change on this count. Basically, to transform the relationship between women and men and people and nature, we need to enhance women's bargaining power in relation to men (both within and outside) the household. Women's bargaining power would depend on three types of interlinked factors-their material situation like independent economic status, economic, social, and political support from external agencies such as kin, the state, and NGO's and gender ideology such as gendered norms and perceptions about women's appropriate roles, rights, abilities, etc.

The gender division of labour depicts power relations and inequalities in work sharing. Men partake in activities that need physical strength and stamina but are seasonal. Men also do activities that have economic value, such as collecting timber and marketing cash crops. Women are attached to activities mainly to sustain invisible and unaccounted livelihoods. There is a gender gap in sharing the workload attached to resources and value. Thus, the gender-differentiated roles and responsibilities in natural resource management and interventions must address the specific needs and opportunities of rural women and men to reduce inequalities, stimulate growth and reverse environmental loss and degradation.

Women may not necessarily be the source of solutions to environmental problems. Groups of women and men may act in environmentally damaging ways. Women's apparent closeness to nature may stem from their lack of opportunities outside the household and social relations in society rather than their biological makeup. Sustainable development, therefore, depends on removing women's subordination, oppression, and poverty, not simply grafting on women as a group or lumping women's varied interests together.

The gender approach to environmental policy should attempt to understand the differences between women and men in households and between subgroups within communities, workloads, use of resources, knowledge and skills, social status, etc. Besides, an attempt should be made to understand power structures and relations, thus recognizing the rights and responsibilities of women and men in communities. These may be partly hidden and may only be obvious with careful investigation. For example, traditional rights of access to land and the products it yields may often be problematic for women as women may not have control over farm products and earnings. These rights might not be written or codified. The socially constructed gender division of labour with women in reproductive, productive, and community organising works gives women less time to invest in their human capital or capacity building for social networking. In general, environmental and resource degradation increases women's workload and drudgery.

The inequalities, as stated above, relate to three aspects: (1) property rights, especially land and forest rights. (2) The gender division of labour; and (3) political authority, power, and access to public decision-making spaces.

## V. Challenges Ahead

Today, there are considerable efforts by environmental academics and activists emphasising the importance of local participation for successful environmental regeneration. As a result, today, we are seeing an emerging consensus among scholars, governments, and NGOs that village communities should manage local resources. However, what shape should community institutions for natural resource management take? Or to what extent can it serve? It is important to probe this since eco-feminism is becoming increasingly important in shaping agendas on women and the environment in international and national forums and among donor agencies.

Several influential environments Thinkers-Carolyn Merchant and Vandana Shiva in South Asia, favour the reviving or replicating of traditional community institutions on the assumption that the past constituted a period of ecological stability and social harmony. Termed by some as the 'new traditionalists,' they represent the pre-colonial period as one of ecological and social culture. Some even consider the entire period from 500 B.C. to A.D. 1860 as relative environmental stability, where caste and associated occupational divisions provided a non-conflictual basis for sharing resources. In that period, communal institutions for resource management are also assumed to have been a common feature. All this, it is argued, was destroyed mostly by colonialism.

Existing evidence provides a very different picture. Undoubtedly, colonialism contributed to an environmental decline in India, especially through large–scale logging for railways, shipbuilding, and plantations, and Statecraft takeovers of forests and communal land, which undermined community property rights and village institutions today. However, the pre–colonial period was far from one of ecological stability, given the growth in human populations and the spread of agriculture. Moreover, although communal resource management institutions did exist, there is little to suggest that these neither were widespread nor can their erosion be attributed only to colonial policies.

Historical representation apart, what is especially problematic in this romanticisation of the past is its uncritical perspective use. Moreover, the revivalist agenda is not confined to a few. According to Gadgil and Guha, in almost all parts of India, social activists of various ideological persuasions - 'Gandhians, Marxists, and wholly apolitical social workers' – seek answers and want to revive traditions.

Notwithstanding and not denying the lessons traditions could offer on some counts, what is at issue here is the inegalitarian social relations and values that most indigenous traditional institutions embody. In endorsing such institutions, there is a striking absence of discussion on their effect on social relations, especially gender relations. Equally, many of the community-based institutional arrangements have emerged in recent years through the encouragement of the government. For example, the Government of Nagaland initiated the concept of communitisation of Public Institutions and Services Acts (2002) in order to build a partnership between the government and the people through the delegation of management responsibilities to the community so that the performance of the public utilities improves in areas such as health, water supply, forest, education, biodiversity, tourism, etc. are found to be entrenched, even exacerbating, gender inequalities.

The gender division of labour continues to be unequal, with women bearing a double work burden. Although women may be allowed to inherit the acquired property, significant inequalities remain, especially concerning ancestral landed property. Despite an improvement in women's education, there is still a wide gap in relation to men at all levels, but especially at higher levels of decision-making. Nagaland has not seen a woman candidate elected for assembly election to date. Furthermore, particularly due to their low representation in decision-making forums (lack of critical mass of women), they have little say in the rules governing natural resource management now being framed. This is a central argument that, although understood by self-respecting development workers and bureaucrats dealing with development, is unfortunately not often brought into the actual policy (Kirpal, 1995).

This neglect of gender in most environmental writing and policy continues, despite the growth of ecofeminist literature. In fact, rather than challenging the traditional view, the premises of ecofeminists tend (however, unwittingly) to reinforce it and thus provide support to institutions and practices that can sustain (or even increase) gender inequalities. Even in the global arena, largely due to ecofeminist advocacy, while the importance of women's role in ecological regeneration is beginning to be recognized, the ground for this recognition is commonly the view that women have a special way of knowing and nurturing nature. So, policy-makers pick up the idea of women's naturalised roles, not rights.

## VI

**Reflection:** Rendering hierarchical structures historically invisibly makes invisible their continuation in the post-colonial period. Today, these forms of inequalities persist, although in less stark forms. We need to consciously transform the formal structures that control natural use and abuse, including existing socio-cultural and political barriers that seem to act as a double-edged sword for Naga womenfolk.

## References

Beauvoir, S. 1949. *The Second Sex*. Translated by H.M. Parshley 1972. Canada: Penguin Books Ltd.

Butler, J. 1990. *Gender Trouble: Feminism and the Subversion of Identity.* New York: Rutledge.

Douglas, Mary. 1970. *Natural Symbols,* Harmondworth: Penguin.

Douglas, Mary. 1988. *Purity and Danger: An Analysis of the Concepts of Pollution and Taboo*, London and New York: Ark Paperbacks. First published 1966.

Escobar, A. 2008.*Territories of Difference: Place, Movement, Life, Redes*. Durham, NC: Duke University Press.

Gadgil & Guha. 1995. *Ecology and Equity*. New Delhi: Penguin Books.

Hubbard, R. 1990. *The Politics of Women's Biology.* New Brunswick: Rutgers University Press.

Kirpal, P. 1995. *Culture and Development*. New Delhi: Har-Anand Publications.

Marion, Y. I. 2002.Lived Body Vs Gender: Reflections on Social Structure and Subjectivity. *Ratio,* 15: 410-428.

Marion, Y. I. 2005. *On Female Body Experience: 'Throwing Like a Girl' and Other Essays*. Oxford University Press.

Merchant, C. 1980. *The Death of Nature: Women, Ecology and the Scientific Revolution.* San Francisco, Harper and Row.

Mies & Shiva, V. 1993. *Ecofeminism.* Delhi: Kali for women.

Moi, T. 2001. *What is a Woman?* New York: Oxford University Press.

Nagaland State Human Development Report (NSHDR). 2004. Department of Planning & Coordination, Government of Nagaland.

Peluso, N.L & Michael, W. 2001. *Violent Environments.* Ithaca & London: Cornell University Press.

Rubin, G. 1975. 'The Traffic in Women: Notes on the Political Economy of Sex'. In R.R. Reiter (ed.), *Towards an Anthropology of Women* 157-210.New York: Monthly Review Press.

Shiva, V.1988. *Staying alive: Women, Ecology and survival.* London: Zed Books.

Tambiah, Stanley J.1970.*Buddhism and the Spirit Cults in North-east Thailand*, London: Cambridge University Press.

Sinha, S., Gururani, S., & Greenberg, B. 1997. The New Traditionalist' Discourse on Indian Environmentalism. *Journal of Peasant Studies*, 24(3): 65-99.

Zehol, L., & Kevekha, K. Z. 2009. *The Legendary Naga Village- A Reader* (Khezhakeno). Dimapur: Heritage Publication House.

# 2

# Cultural adaptation and Coping mechanism of Domestic Water supply in Yikhum village of Nagaland

**Longshibeni N. Kithan**

The present study contextualises the Lotha Naga tribe of Yikhum Village in Nagaland. Like many tribal societies, the social system of the Lothas at micro, meso, and macro levels is fast evolving, giving rise to newer forms of cultural adaptation and coping mechanisms. The domain of water is no exception. Recently, the state government has intervened to facilitate water quality and quantity concerns. At the village level, decentralisation of domestic water services is institutionalised through the Water and Sanitation Committee (WATSAN). Since WATSAN intervened, changes have been observed in the delivery of water services. Attempting a holistic stance and by tracing the historical process of decentralisation, the present chapter, therefore, emphasises upon its effectiveness to provide domestic water supply.

## Introduction

Water is perceived and valued differently in different contexts associated with their cultural beliefs, norms, and practices playing a big part in shaping them. They implicate how water is managed, whether revered or abused (Strang, 2004). For instance, in the Indian subcontinent, several theoretical, analytical and empirical research depicts strong human- water relationship (Jain et al, 2018; Malik, S, 2016; Nair, 2004). Citing Hastings (1977), Kumar and Katara says, that the people's belief system in ancient India accentuates sacredness and curative aspects of water. Furthermore, they take the readers back to the Vedic period through the ancient Indian scriptures like the Rig Veda, Yajur Veda, Atharva Veda and others, to tell that these sources suggest strong water themes in relation to its symbolism, divinities, performance of rituals, natural phenomena such as water cycle, cloud formation, stream flow, water table, and hydraulic machines etc. They also refer to important civilisations like the Indus Valley Civilisation (derived from the river Indus) that not only tells about the significance of water for development of civilisation but was also known for their efficient water and sanitation management practices. The Mauryan empire that followed also had unique dams which were inspired by people's socio-economic and religious way of life.

Recent contemporary water struggles in different contexts suggest changing conceptualisation of water. For instance, Singh (2006) analyzed the symbolic meaning of water use and management in rural central eastern Bihar and central Madhya Pradesh and found out that water is encoded with sacred and secular values. In the sacred domain particularly, water is associated with 'purity' and 'pollution' binary. In this sense, the upper caste members in the social hierarchy were restrained from utilising water used by the lower caste, which was considered contaminated. Consequently, they adhere to them because violation of the order is likely to invite supernatural consequences. In other forms of struggles, Mosse (2003) provides an ethnography of an ancient tank irrigation system in two villages in the Ramnad district of Southern Tamil Nadu. He shows how social and political factors influence and interact with the ecology of water flows in the tank irrigation system. Building his argument on fieldwork, oral histories, and detailed archival work, he is perplexed at how certain political entities have historically exercised their control by diverting river water and the layout of channels and drainage.

Elsewhere, Strang (2013) analyzes differential perception from water damming in the Upper Murray darling basin, Australia. The dam's construction is the epitome of success and sustainability for the upstream communities. At the same time, it is corrupt capitalism and a catastrophe for humans, flora, and fauna for the downstream communities. In addition, Limbert (2001) analyzes shifting perception owing to adopting newer water supply systems like water pipes, electric coolers, and diesel in an Omani town. These new systems made it possible to commoditise water by privileging water ownership to private parties. Furthermore, people lost the deep connection and hindered memories that they shared with traditional water systems, and this void was particularly pronounced among the older generations.

Singh, with her team of researchers, provides another ethnographic account of three states of India, viz., Bihar, Jharkhand, and Madhya Pradesh, and argues for the failure of the newly installed modern hand pump system.

They found that the lack of holistic consideration of multiple actors' perspectives, particularly women's concern in planning and management, was a major hurdle. The hand pump system, supposed to ease the burden of women, was only received as an additional service with not many benefits in terms of comfort, better health, and enhancement of socio-economic conditions, hence inadequate to address the needs of the people (Singh et al., 2004). On the contrary, however, Espejo (1993) shows how the emphasis on gender balance in domestic water management resulted in clear benefits in terms of improved delivery of water services, sanitation, and economic empowerment. In this case, the low-income women in Urban Honduras provide water to various households through licenced water vending points. They were also given a choice to decide the cost of water, and the income generated from selling water was utilised for household expenditure and other community development activities. In another form of conflict resolution, the Berbers of the High Atlas Mountains and Bedouins of the Negev desert practice a significant way of resolving conflict: '*Sulha.*' in which people believing in the doctrine of forgiveness, which Islam propagates, observe a special ceremony to commemorate the absolution of old grudges (Wolf, 2000). Newer studies in India and outside India suggest the effectiveness of traditional rainwater harvesting, community participation and decentralisation in the light of contemporary challenges (Daigger, 2009; Opare, 2012).

These are a few examples that suggest how culture influences perception, value and management of water, and discusses varied struggles, conflict and coping with water in different contexts. Drawing lessons from the existing body of work, the present chapter also attempts to navigate the case of a rural domestic water system.

The present study was undertaken among the Lotha Nagas of Yikhum village in the Wokha district of Nagaland for the historical and cultural relevance for the study. Further, it is an excerpt from the Author's Doctoral thesis. Household census, oral narratives, key informants, interviews (one to one and focus group) and longtime ethnographic observations are the sources of data, and thematic and content analysis was undertaken for the data gathered.

## Traditional beliefs, value and management of water

To achieve a holistic overview, the management, value and perception among the Lothas of Yikhum village need to be looked at in the light of past and ongoing events. Primarily, a brief profile of the village is that

Yikhum village is recognised to be one of the oldest villages in the Lotha area. According to Census 2011, the village has a total household population of 461 with 3,174 people, of which the male population is 1,571 and females constitute 1,603. The literacy rate of Yikhum village is 63.23%, of which 67.60% of males and 58.95% of females are literate. In addition, Yikhum village is located in Englan circle of Wokha district in Nagaland, India, which lies about 16 km from sub-district Englan (tehsildar office) and 16 km from district headquarters Wokha where major economic activities occur.

In Yikhum, the major domestic water sources are natural springs, streams, rivers, and natural rainwater. These water sources are found in individual-owned, clan, and community/village land. Earlier, water was obtained directly from these natural sources, and women undertook the task of collecting and managing water at home. During dry months, women must walk long distances, often far from the village settlement, to collect water. Now, people can bring water close to or at home through water pipes and a common tap water system introduced by the State government departments.

Traditionally, water was considered a gift from the creator among the Lothas, meant to be shared and harnessed for free. If any household in the village is deprived of water, the entire community would collectively resolve the matter. Deprivation of water to any household is a matter of shame. As a result, there was never a conscious instance when the water storage of one emptied and that of the other overflowed with water, and the concept of buying and selling water was unknown. If at all they occur, they will be checked, and efforts will be made to tackle them individually and collectively. In addition, an individual consciously avoids open defecation in and around water bodies and improper waste disposal. Their non-adherence was again checked and penalised befittingly by the *tongti* (Council of knowledgeable elderly men). The *tongti* would also mobilise the entire community for water source maintenance and impart adequate sanitation practices.

Water preservation was also prompted by fear of spiritual or supernatural misfortune, which was tied with the Lothas Animistic tradition. The associated resources in the forest were regarded as the abode of spirits, namely *sükhyingo, tsün-grham,* and *lüngkumvü.* They had minimal human disturbance, including felling trees, cutting and clearing jungles for fear of likely misfortune for the community. As a result, these misfortunes would not befall them in the form of little or no rainfall. Thus, when an individual falls a tree, water is poured in and around where the tree had been felled.

By doing so, they would eventually succeed in reconciliation and withhold the wrath of the spirits.

Significantly this interaction of humans, nature, and the supernatural realm could be further placed into perspective by Vidyarthi's 'man-nature spirit complex.' Whereby the natural environment is weaved with human social organisation. The dependency and reverence for water and other associated natural resources prompt activities that propitiate numerous deities or spirits who are believed to dwell in these natural spaces. Any effort to abstain from acts considered profane was part of the larger scheme of attachment that they hold with the natural environment and spirit realm, eventually resulting in conservation and environmental protection.

However, social and natural environment change impacts the conception, value, and management of water. In turn, cultural adaptation has implications, leading to the vulnerability of traditional knowledge. For example, the sacredness and reverence towards water have lessened in the recent times. In view of this, it is significant to mention that the Lotha Nagas, like any other Naga tribe, in the past had and continue to negotiate the newer elements due to the colonial legacy and post-colonial Indian state, notwithstanding the resonance of global forces. The Lotha Nagas were earlier self-governing independent units prior to their entrance otherwise.

To elaborate further about the contemporary changes, for household utility, modern tap water systems were introduced with the intervention of the state government department PHED. While it enabled the people to bring water close to home other than physically fetching it from long distances, newer challenges have arisen. In addition, exposure to market forces introduces the idea of commoditisation, and there is now a choice to buy and sell water when required during special events by wealthy households, in particular creating a disparity between those who can pay for water and those who cannot, although this magnitude of commoditisation may not necessarily be at par with urban experience. Furthermore, the institution of *tongti* which now comes within the larger ambit of the Village council, and WATSAN falling within its purview, also brought new changes. The governing principles, that is community participation, however, remain almost the same in both the former and the latter; only state patronage is evident in the latter. Again, aspects of traditional animistic belief that binds them with nature and the supernatural realm leading to the preservation of natural resources, has lessened. Although some scholars associated the adoption of the Christian faith as an influencing factor in this form of cultural adaptation, there is no mutual agreement among scholars since the philosophical premise of the Biblical scriptures does not endorse human exploitative behaviour whatsoever.

The above description is only a gist of the current changes, but the transitions are evident on the whole, and it has a bearing on the traditional conception, valuation, and management of water. However, it is also significant to take cognisance of the region's complex socio-political, historical and political process as a whole and holistically prior to arriving at any sweeping generalisations on the Lothas.

## Decentralisation of domestic water supply

Concept of decentralisation has evolved over the years. Despite this, there is a general acceptance, globally, about certain characteristics, that is greater participation, less bureaucratic and increased flexibility and accountability in decentralisation. Research suggests that, while decentralisation could be applied to different contexts, it must consider the varying contextual factors, capacity, and power dynamics for successful implementation. In the Indian context, decentralisation dates back to pre-independence era, and it was a product of various political, social and economic factors (Chakraborthy et al., 2017). Coming to Nagaland, ensuring delivery of basic services and everyday utilities has been an utmost concern in the last few decades since the formation of statehood in 1963. Further, the State Government instituted the Nagaland communitisation of Public Institutions and Services Act in 2002 to empower and ensure local participation in education, health, water supply, roads, power, sanitation, forests, and other welfare and development schemes. Nevertheless, it does not mean to suggest that there was a lack of people's involvement in the traditional social system as discussed above. Instead, the author argues that the institution of decentralisation has been strengthened by best practices of the past, with the patronage it received from the State government.

> "Governments worldwide need to break with 'business as usual' and engage in ever more innovative ways of delivering public services and organising how they function. Your exemplary initiatives should inspire all governments around the world at all levels to strive for excellence in public service".

The then Deputy Secretary General of the United Nations (2005- 2012) made this statement in appreciation for Nagaland's communitisation of Public Institutions and Services, which received a coveted United Nations award for public service in New York on 23 June 2008 from Asia and the

Pacific region. This award was in recognition of the contribution made in policy through innovative means and for elevating the state towards fulfilling Millennium Development goals. Furthermore, pooled from over a hundred nominations across the globe, only twelve organisations were finally selected in three different categories. (Rediff.com, June 24, 2008).

Before decentralisation, waterworks was initiated by the state government departments such as the Public Works Department and Department of Rural Development. The domain of domestic water was later handed over to the Public Health Engineering Department (PHED), which bifurcated from the Public Works Department. In addition, since water management entails land issue settlement, the government can only initiate water development works in consultation with the people. In view of this, when PHED began its operation in Yikhum village, it experienced numerous difficulties. Winning the people's trust was a herculean task because prior development experience, particularly land acquisition, was not favourable to the people. Despite difficulties and following repeated arbitration, a mutual consensus was later possible, and water work began.

Water tanks were constructed during the first phase to store water for supply to the villagers. During this phase, people immediately developed huge expectations, but it was short-lived since there needed to be more improvement in the delivery of water services. Water supply was unpredictable most of the time and, when available, was insufficient to meet daily basic requirements. Furthermore, water pipes would also succumb to leakages and breakages before reaching the village from the main reservoir, and many women continue to walk long distances to fetch water. In worst circumstance, the problem would be left unattended for days together and even months long. In addition, sanitation and hygiene were neglected since most households need proper toilets and open defecation, and improper waste disposal practices were rampant.

Following the unsatisfactory attempts of the PHED, decentralisation through WATSAN finally began in Yikhum village on 7th August 2005. Since then, remarkable improvement in the delivery of water supply and sanitation has been observed. WATSAN functions in consultation with the village council and PHED, and they undertake tasks such as operation and maintenance of water supply, tackling the land issue, if any, collecting water fees, and looking after sanitation matters. The village members nominate WATSAN members with the village council's approval for five years. Currently, six members comprise a chairman, a secretary, and representatives from all four khels, with no female representative.

Furthermore, the accounts provided by ordinary villagers, village leaders, knowledgeable elderly people, and WATSAN has been analyzed to discuss the effectiveness of decentralisation through WATSAN. In this case, the parameter adopted are accountability, accessibility and justice, affordability, sanitation needs, and lessened land issues.

## Accountability

The water and sanitation key actors, such as PHED, WATSAN, and Village Council, are accountable for one another's activities. They are bound to work in consultation with one another and function as a team. PHED would maintain a record of all their interventions and utilisation of funds within a particular scheme and submit an audit report on completing their work to the funding agency. Furthermore, PHED would receive regular updates about the fund utilisation from the WATSAN. WATSAN, in turn, keeps the village members informed about all their activities. They are open to those who wish to obtain information pertaining to financial matters. WATSAN committee would even convene a separate meeting for the same purpose at regular intervals.

Despite many efforts, there were a few instances when trivial arguments broke between the villagers and WATSAN on alleged misappropriation of funds, but they were resolved amicably without escalating. Other than them, no major argument was known.

## Accessibility and justice

WATSAN committee ascertained that the water supply from PHED is accessible to all households. In order to ensure this, several steps were undertaken. The water tap was installed within reach of two different khels. Necessary information was given concerning the time of water's flow to prevent excess water flow. The households that can afford direct individual piped water supply for home use can do so without hindrance. PHED workers commissioned by the villagers provide their service to such intending households without any labour cost except for water pipes and other essential machinery. For sanitation purposes, community toilets and waste bins are placed in several locations in the village.

In addition, WATSAN ensures the maintenance of discipline and any likelihood of unfair practices that may arise while delivering basic domestic water supply and sanitation. For example, deliberate efforts are made to ensure that no household is favoured above the other. They see people standing in queues waiting to fill their buckets whenever water is made available to the villagers through several water outlets. If the decorum is hindered and results in conflicts, they often resolve on mutual understanding between the two opposing parties. In extreme cases, the WATSAN physically intervenes and delivers justice.

As such, there was no shortage of efforts from the WATSAN except for the naturally induced shortages, particularly during non-rainy months, often outside their control. For instance, water from *sangphya* and *kesutong,* which serve as the significant natural water sources of supply for the village, dries up during the non-rainy months. In addition, although the WATSAN committee expressed their desire to build additional water tanks in the village to increase water storage, it could not materialise due to lack of adequate funds.

## Lessened land issue

One of the major hindrances faced by PHED while executing water development work in Yikhum is the land issue. Since WATSAN intervened, the land issue has lessened considerably. For example, WATSAN mediates between PHED and the village members when a water project involves land negotiation. WATSAN would communicate with the people about the larger purpose and reliability of work and assure adequate compensation to those landowners whose land is to be compromised. On many occasions, people have readily cooperated with WATSAN. Few have even offered to donate immovable property like individual land for water development work. Currently, one of the main tanks in the village is built on land donated by an individual household. Otherwise, it would not have occurred if PHED had intervened directly.

## Sanitation

Water and sanitation are interrelated because if anything goes wrong, later compromise the former. WATSAN takes cognisance of people's sanitation needs. During the initial phase of decentralisation, WATSAN distributed around 100 commodes to the village members. It is noteworthy that most households in the village have built proper toilets and waste disposal bins. WATSAN has contributed six community dustbins, placed in all four khels for proper waste disposal. WATSAN also built six community toilets in different village locations to avoid open defecation. In addition, the committee also undertakes sensitisation programmes on the importance of sanitation and hygiene during community gatherings.

## Affordability

In Yikhum village, the water fee is both fixed and voluntary. In the case of a fixed fee, the WATSAN decided on the minimum water fee in consultation with the PHED. Presently, the water fee is imposed only on households with direct access to water from the main tank of PHED. They are obliged to pay a compulsory sum of Rupees 50 per month. Water fees may also be fixed at any time for all households other than an individual connection at regular intervals. It may range between Rupees 50-300. Consensus with the village member takes place while deciding the fees. In addition, the other kind of water fee is the voluntary contribution of the individual household. The monetary collection gathered in the process is utilised to meet the cost of basic repair work, lessening the burden and the long wait for technical assistance from PHED. Significantly, households of older people were exempted from fees. On the whole, the villagers thought that the fee was minimal and affordable, with many expressing the willingness to pay higher sums for better water access, particularly during dry months and so long as the money is utilised efficiently for the community's welfare.

## Problematising gender imbalances in decision making

Another significant theme pursued in domestic water in recent times is in relation to women's contribution in domestic water management. In rural areas, it is mainly women who collect, manage and ensure equitable water distribution for various purposes at home. In this sense, the skills and knowledge acquired in the process are remarkable and undisputed. However, more women's underrepresentation in important decisions regarding water is equally concerning and picking up trends. Although there are clear benefits associated with raising women's voice in water decision-making, many scholars have attributed traditional norms normalising women's incapacitation in the public sphere as a barrier (Wegerich & Warner; Zwarteveen, 2008, Maharaj, 2003).

In the context of the Lotha Nagas of Yikhum village, the decentralisation through WATSAN has yet to involve women in the WATSAN committees effectively. This is because WATSAN needed more female representatives to ensure their effective participation.

In a casual conversation one Sunday afternoon, Informant X (name disguised), 49 said,

> *"What water skill women possibly acquire by mere fetching and distribution of water for various activities within the household, it is*

*men who initiate all important decisions concerning water and sanitation. Moreover, we do not want our women to leave aside household chores and running around in the village repairing broken water pipes*."

The WATSAN Chairman then added to the conversation and remarked,

*"I do not see any issue with women's underrepresentation in the committee. If there is any, PHED representatives should have pursued it"*.

On another occasion, Informant Y (Name disguised), a female villager of 44 years of age, says,

*"We are expected not to speak authoritatively to men*."

Statements such as these were common, revealing the issue's mundanity so much that women's underrepresentation does not evoke a sense of urgency to respond. Certainly, the normalisation of patriarchal notions and practices for men and women has overshadowed women's position. Both men and women are not particularly motivated to break traditional barriers that appear to sabotage them. Oftentimes they do not realise that they are even being sabotaged. This, however, means that the contribution of women still needs to be improved. Presently, women in the village continue to collect and manage equitable water distribution for various purposes. It is used for sacred purposes by partial or full immersion during the conferring of blessings and repenting of sins among the Christian Lothas; for a basic utility like drinking, cooking, cleaning, and washing and for productive purposes like crop cultivation and pig rearing. In addition, the money generated in the process of selling crops and pig rearing is diversifying livelihood opportunities. Owing to their close engagement physically or otherwise, they are equipped to represent their priorities and aspirations effectively like anywhere else.

Given the above, it becomes relevant to ask whether the celebrated traditional norms, because it is non-exploitative, are justified here. Significantly, it was also observed that besides the traditional normalisation of women's underrepresentation in the public sphere, there needed to be more awareness of the possible benefits of women's participation in important water decisions. No sensitisation and awareness programmes were known in the village, whether initiated by WATSAN or other local bodies when the study was conducted. In this context, it may be logical to wait to see any changes if awareness and sensitisation are created in the foreseeable future. Undeniably though, traditional norms that created a disparity between men and women regarding influence in the public sphere have not changed despite the institutionalisation of supposedly an improvised participatory mechanism.

## Conclusion

The above discussion analyzed the cultural adaptation and water coping mechanisms. The author points out how the traditional perception, value, and management of water reflect reverence, thereby influencing conservation efforts individually and collectively. There on, she argues about the changing human-water relationship, which further needs to be analyzed in the light of the region's complex socio-cultural, historical and political process, of which the Lotha Nagas are a part. Nagaland government decentralisation initiative since its inception has resulted in accessibility, affordability, accountability, enhanced sanitation, and lessening of land issues, which were observed and perceived to be beneficial by the villagers. In this sense, the author sees these efforts as strengthening the traditional institutions, values and practices. On the other hand, the correlation between women and water management which has been enhanced with the increasing recognition of women's skills and knowledge in the water domain in recent times, the author attempts to understand this recognition and maximize the potential of women's representation in decision-making. Considering multi-layered (holistically), the author concludes that a traditional norm of men in decision-making should be analyzed to advance more nuanced thoughts and actions inclusively and sustainably.

## References

Chakraborthy, P; Chakraborthy, L; & Mukherjee, A. (2017). *Social sector in a decentralised economy- India in the era of Globalisation.* Cambridge University press.

Daigger, G. T. (2009). Evolving Urban water and residuals management paradigms: Water reclamation and reuse, decentralisation and resource recovery. *Water environment research, Vol. 81*(8), 809-823.

Espejo, N. (1993). Action learning, building on experience.

Jain, K.S., Lohani, A.K., Khobragade, S. D., Singh, P.K., Ullah, F., & Pandey, C. (2018). *Hydrologic knowledge in ancient India (Second edition).* National Institute of Hydrology, Roorkee, India.

Kumar, S. & Katara, S. (2021). Ancient knowledge of water and water traditions in India. The Discussant. ISSN 2250-3412. *Centre for reforms, development and Justice. Vol. III* (4), 36-49.

Limbert, M.E. (2001). The senses of Water in an Omani town. *Social text* 68, 19(3), 35-55.

Malik, S. (2016). Conceptual aspect of Hydrological cycle in India mythology of Kishkindhakanda Ramayan. *Journal of Environment and Earth science, 6* (4).

Mosse, D. (2003). *The rule of Water: Statecraft, ecology and collective action in south India.* New Delhi: Oxford University Press.

Nair, K.S. (2004). *Role of water in the development of Civilisation in India- a review of ancient literature, traditional practices and beliefs.* The basis of civilisation-water science (Proceedings of the UNESCO, IAHS, IWI Symposium, 2003), Rome: IAHS publication.

Opare, S. (2012). Rainwater harvesting: An option for sustainable rural water supply in Ghana. *Geo Journal, Vol. 77* (5), 695-705.

Singh, N. (2006). Indigenous water management systems- interpreting symbolic dimensions in common property resource regimes. *Society and natural resources,* 19 (4), 357-366

Singh, N., Bhatacharya, P., Jacks, G., & Gustafsson, J.E. (2004). Women and modern domestic water supply systems: Need for a holistic perspective. *water resources management,* 18, 237-248.

Strang, V. (2004). The meaning of Water. New york: Berg publisher.

Strang, V. (2013). Dam nation: CUbbie station and the waters of the Darling. In J. Wagner (Eds.), *The social life of water in a time of crisis* (pp. 36-60). New York: Berghahn.

Wolf, A.T. (2000). Indigenous approaches to water conflict negotiations and implications for international waters.

# 3

# Women and Indigenous Knowledge of Rice

**Khachungla Tangvah**

**Abstract**

Traditionally rice cultivation have been a women's domain of knowledge among the Tangkhuls. The wide array of varieties of rice found in the village reflects vast knowledge of seeds from the women. Moreover, women have developed complex systems of pests' management and biological control. They have identified and managed a series of rice varieties suitable for different soil types. For example, for seeds germination and preventing the crops from insect/pest attack in the field and during the storage, they would apply their rich traditional knowledge. Women, who are the custodians of seeds, are also responsible for their selection. They are the repositories of this knowledge and, in a true sense, owners of this complex seed technology and expertise. This paper discusses the indigenous knowledge and technologies used by the farmers in rice cultivation with special emphasis on jhum and terrace cultivations of Khambi and Nungbi Khullen village of Ukhrul district, Manipur. Fieldwork was carried out during two agricultural cycles, and the study is empirical and exploratory.

**Keywords:** Folk Knowledge, Indigenous Knowledge, Local Knowledge, Rice Culture, Traditional Knowledge, Women Knowledge.

## Introduction

Rice grain is produced in a wide range of locations under various climatic conditions, from the wettest areas in the world to the driest deserts. It is the second most widely consumed cereal crop in the world, next to wheat. It is also considered as an ancient crop; archaeological evidence predates any literary evidence on rice culture. The growth stage of the rice crop marks the passage of time and seasons. It permeates all aspects of the culture of the people who consume rice as their main food. In India as a whole, rice has enjoyed unique status since ancient times because of its special attributes, such as vitality, vigour, and rice as a means of fulfillment of all ends in life. From the vast array of agricultural products, rice plays a significant role in the traditional Indian village economy. However, money seems to have played a minimal role in the economy, due to the cash shortage and the absence of proper markets. A review of archaeological findings of the Indus-Saraswati civilisation shows that they ate wild rice in the advanced Mesolithic or pre-Neolithic period. Although its exact place, time of origin, and the earliest cultivation of rice were not known, it was found mentioned in the Hindu Vedas, Samhitas, Puranas, Kautilya's *Arthasastra,* Krishi-Parashara, Buddhist and Jain literature (Nene, 2005; Prasad, 2012; Kumar, 1988; Smith, 2006). Yet, uncertainties or deficiencies in history, archaeological and anthropological studies have obscured the time and place of the earliest cultivation of rice.

Indigenous knowledge of rice has been passed from generation to generation, usually through oral communication and cultural rituals. It has been the basis for agriculture, food preparation and conservation, healthcare, education, and a wide range of other activities that sustain a society and its environment in many parts of the world for many centuries (Senanayake, 2006). Indigenous knowledge of rice is a unique knowledge confined to a particular culture or society. It is also known as local knowledge, folk knowledge, people's knowledge, traditional wisdom, or traditional science. This knowledge is generated and transmitted by communities, over time, to cope with their agroecological and socio-economic environments (Fernandez, 1994). It is generated through a systematic process of observing local conditions, experimenting with solutions, and readapting previously identified solutions to modified environmental, socio-economic, and technological situations (Brouwers, 1993). Indigenous knowledge is found to be socially desirable, economically, affordable, sustainable, and involves minimal risk. Farmers-based indigenous/traditional knowledge has a scientific rationale and relevance for agricultural productivity and sustainability.

Traditionally, rice cultivation have been a women's domain of knowledge among the Tangkhuls. The wide array of varieties of rice found in the village reflects vast knowledge of seeds from the women. Moreover, women have developed complex systems of pests' management and biological control. Today, there is a grave risk that much indigenous knowledge is being lost and, along with it, valuable knowledge about ways of living sustainably both ecologically and socially. Indigenous knowledge systems have not been systematically recorded in written form and are not readily accessible to agricultural researchers, development practitioners, and policymakers.

Recently some workers have shown an interest in indigenous knowledge. However, still, there is a grave risk that much indigenous knowledge is being lost and, along with it, valuable knowledge about ways of living sustainably both ecologically and socially. Therefore, this paper attempts to provide readers with the indigenous knowledge of rice in the sustainable development process and encourage academics, policymakers, scientists, and students to gain enhanced respect for local culture, its wisdom, and its environmental ethics.

## Study Area

Khambi (Jhum) and Nungbi Khullen (Terraced) villages were selected for the present study. These two villages were selected from two geographical locations from southern (Khambi) and northern (Nungbi Khullen) zones where jhum and terraced paddy cultivations were prominently practiced, respectively. Khambi is a village situated in Phungyar Block of Ukhrul district in Manipur. The village has 112 families. According to Census 2011, Khambi's population is 642. Out of this, 333 are males while the females count 309 here. Literacy rate is 56 percent. The village is 86 km away from the district headquarter. The village is the home of the Tangkhul Naga Tribes. Nungbi Khullen is a village situated in Chingai Block of Ukhrul district in Manipur. It is from the northern zone under Chingai Block known as Raphei by the Tangkhuls. The village is 36 km away from the district headquarter. The village consists of 352 houses with a total population of 1602 as per Population Census 2011. Literacy rate in Nungbi Khullen village is 55 percent. This village is one of the biggest villages under Chingai Block.

## Method of Study

The study is based on both primary and secondary sources. Observation played an important role. Observing the people in the religious festivals, rituals, food habits, social organisation, economy, and their day-to-day life gives enormous data on the indigenous knowledge of agriculture, particularly rice in Tangkhuls life. Extensive interviews and discussions were also done with the local community members and holders of traditional knowledge and wisdom, which form the basis of this research work. Besides, books and journals, magazines, etc., were consulted for supplementing the article.

## Results and Discussion Indigenous knowledge of rice as medicine

Rice is still used as a medicinal substance during childbirth and illnesses by the local people. Whenever a person is sick, a kind of porridge-like locally called *zatkapet* is served. For diarrhoea-suffering patients, *kaporla khamui*, bread made of red rice, is given. For any deadly attack like insects, bees, etc., especially a snake's bite, and for any food poisoning from eating wild fruits, leaves, roots, mushrooms, etc., rice beer is given. A small stripe, made of paddies, soaked for three to four days, wrapped in a wet cloth, and dried in the sun for a few days, becomes an effective medicine locally known as *havu* (yeast) in brewing rice beer. A small portion of this *havu* stripe is put in the rice beer brewing pot. This *havu* determines the hardness of the rice beer, and it is the *havu* that gives the taste and resistance power to any poisonous attack. Even today, it is widely used as first aid for its effectiveness and maybe because of its easy availability.

Indigenous medical practitioners tackle prevention as well as therapy, perceiving illness and healing holistically. Therapies often enhance healing by treating the whole being, rather than targeting specific symptoms, and trace the disease to the context of the person's life.

## Indigenous knowledge of rice as cosmetics and others

Tangkhul women have used rice water as a hair treatment for centuries. Traditionally, soaked rice water, before cooking called *samra*, and a grease type of wild leaf locally called *hamnen* served as hair shampoo. This *samra* is also used as a soap for the body. A few women said that *samra* (soaked rice water) is very good for skin and long hair. It keeps the hair smooth, thick, and lasting. Rice flour is also used by quarters of women in the village as face packs to lighten their skin complexion, make the skin fair, tone, remove the dead skin cells, etc.

Weaving is another important industry of the Tangkhuls. They make varieties of shawls, and loincloths for both men and women. Local people use rice to make weaving smoother; where rice is boiled, and thoroughly stirred; this sticky flour is good for dyeing the weaving materials before weaving. Again the husks and straw of the rice are best for soil manure. Thus, rice was the most commonly used item, from food to cosmetics. However, this wide array of traditional rice knowledge is on the verge of extinction as younger generations use other market products. Because people have now neither used nor have any awareness of this indigenous idea. Besides, the researcher hardly met people using *samra,* except a few older women. When they were asked to say any differences between the *samra* and modern shampoo/soap, they exclamator said: "*Oih Aayaha*! *Samra* is far better than the market shampoo. What is going on? Today's youngsters' even small kids have grey hair and lesser hair, everything buys in the money". It reflects their preference towards the use of rice for washing hair than the market shampoo.

A number of researchers conducted a research project entitled, 'Rice water: A traditional ingredient with anti-aging efficacy'. A small study with 12 participants tested a rice water gel on the skin for 28 days. The researchers found that the rice had the same antioxidant activity as ascorbic acid (Marto, et al., 2018). Marto et al. stated, "Rice water should be thus considered as an anti-aging ingredient to be used in skincare products."

Modern scientists have also developed various cosmetics and anti-aging supplements from rice bran, like 'rice brightening scrub,' and 'rice ceramide,' etc. Rice bran has been widely used in manufacturing medicines, cosmetics, and anti-aging supplements for women as well as being used as a supplement to help develop muscles in the body, to increase strength.

## Women and indigenous knowledge of rice

Indigenous knowledge in agriculture is very vast and diverse. This knowledge of rice has been collected, accumulated, and perfected over centuries. Indigenous knowledge of the people is very effective in meeting their food requirements in areas of land clearing, sowing, harvesting, weeding, etc. Their mixed farming, mixed cropping, crop rotation, etc., helped tremendously in their bumper harvest. Indigenous crops of a particular area play a vital role in food security. Local people of Ukhrul use varieties of indigenous crops. Indigenous knowledge systems have a broad perspective of the ecosystems and of sustainable ways of using natural resources.

Women of jhum and terrace cultivators identify varieties of paddy used by them. The women carry this knowledge of paddy and its varieties wherever they go, even when they marry a man of another village. For instance, the *Kasuipui* paddy variety was brought by a girl from *Kasho* village who married a man of Khambi village (Tangvah, 2017). Certain native varieties have distinct cultural or religious values and were used during certain social events and ceremonies. Women have not only developed complex systems of pests' management and biological control, but they have identified and managed a series of paddy varieties suitable for different soil types. For instance, the jhum cultivators use *takansang, mayneh*, and *sangpu* varieties in fertile soil, as these types of plants are short in height.

Moreover, in a fertile field, if they plant a tall variety of paddy, it may fall before the harvest, and thus the crop may get damaged. For infertile soil, they use tall varieties of paddy such as *mahungsang* and *kasuipu.* In thick forest land, which usually has a colder climate, *charapu* and *mahungsang* were cultivated. Sticky rice like *lara, larathao,* and *athao* are good in warmer climatic conditions. They identify paddy that can be used in fertile and infertile soil, such as *lamyang* and *changlai*. Women *jhumia* change the varieties of the paddy depending on the 'plot site' of the year. Terrace women cultivators used *rachotra, changkuila*; *kaporla* in cold water and; *utaipi, rashemti*, and *makri* in warmer land. They used *hunemla, haneila*, and s*hempom* varieties in fertile soil, as these plants are short. Women, who are the custodians of seeds, are also responsible for their selection (Fig. 1, 2 and 3). They are the repositories of this knowledge and, in a true sense, owners of this complex seed technology and knowledge. Despite women's rich heritage of farming experiences, they are ridiculed by a common saying that "hen's knowledge is more farsighted than the women's knowledge". (Tangvah, 2017).

**Fig. 1: A woman preparing for seed sowing.**

**Fig. 2: View of women transplanting the paddies.**

**Fig. 3: Women weeding the paddies.**

## Use of Indigenous Knowledge in Sustainable Development Process

Our policymakers need to recognize the value of participatory approaches in decision-making for sustainable development. Indigenous knowledge provides the basis for grassroots decision-making. It has been recently found that the indigenous knowledge of ecological zones, natural resources, agriculture, aquaculture, forest, and game management is far more sophisticated than previously assumed (Posey, 1995). Furthermore, this knowledge offers new models for development that are both ecologically and socially sound. Therefore, it is a well-known fact that development activities that work with and through indigenous knowledge have several important advantages over projects that operate outside them. One classic example is reverting to 'non-scientific' polyculture (mixed cropping) from 'scientific' monoculture. The characteristics of traditional polycultures that make them desirable were ignored by agricultural researchers in developing countries, introducing the concept of the green revolution into those countries. But recently, research concerning polycultures has blossomed, and some of their benefits are becoming clear. Polyculture is the sustainable farming system that has prevailed in Khambi and Nungbi Khullen for more than a hundred years.

It has many sustainable characteristics such as low pest and disease incidences, efficient use of labour, intensification of production with limited natural resources, and maximisation of returns under low levels of technology. The local people have acquired this knowledge through millennia of accumulated experience and survival are invaluable in designing modern development plans. Therefore, the policymakers should pay greater attention to indigenous knowledge in the development process at a policy level.

The vast majority of the population in the Ukhrul district is small-scale farmers, each working less than two hectares of land. They search for solutions for their 'localised' farming problems through indigenous knowledge. Such technology is user-derived and tested through time. On the other hand, the critical strength of indigenous knowledge is its ability to see the inter-relation of disciplines and then integrate them meaningfully. This holistic perspective and the resulting synergism show higher developmental impact, adaptability, and sustainability levels than modern knowledge. Therefore, it is an excellent source of readily available and already tested appropriate technology for policymakers to use in their planning process. The value of indigenous knowledge is not only limited to agriculture, the environment, and biodiversity. It has an immense value in other fields such as education, medicine, etc. In the 1990s, the realisation is gradually dawning that women have a right to be directly involved in the decision-making process that affects their lives and offer society insights, skills, and talents that differ from those of men. One of the spheres where such differences are most evident is indigenous knowledge (Fernandez, 1994).

## Conclusion

This study has shown that women's traditional knowledge activities applied in the rice cultivation and post-harvesting processing of rice are vital (See Fig. 4, 5, 6, 7 and 8). Without this, the final product would be gritty, rough, and compromised. It discusses the key role of women as holders of local and indigenous knowledge and as agents of change and community cohesion at the local level. It also highlights women's transmission, preservation, and elaboration of local knowledge related to sustainable development, biodiversity, and climate change. Indeed, women are frequently the primary managers of rice, collectors of natural resources such as drinking water, fuel, or small agroforestry plots, medicinal plants, and the primary holders of knowledge concerning such resources.

Women in the study areas are more active than men in rice farming activities. As such, it is unlikely that my research will achieve its full potential without the inclusion of women at all levels. Increasingly, it has been recognised that men do not and possibly cannot express essential aspects of women's experience and interests (Moser, 1993). As such, women's knowledge must be considered separately from that of men.

There is much to be learned from the indigenous knowledge systems of local people. All academics, policymakers, planners should pay greater attention to this invaluable treasure of knowledge threatened by extinction. Suppose we are to move towards interactive technology development from the conventional transfer of technology approach. In that case, we all may have to learn many things from our village-level experts, the master of indigenous knowledge. Innovation in indigenous knowledge systems must be encouraged so that individuals can find new opportunities to mitigate the effects of the scarcity of natural resources, drought, and unfavourable market conditions. If indigenous knowledge systems are to continue to contribute to the quest for sustainable development, their capacity to focus on diversity and locality as well as to innovate based on gendered-knowledge-generating processes must be recognised and respected.

Women are the backbone of the community and play a crucial role in the preservation of food security. They also have a fundamental collective and community role as guardians of indigenous ancestral knowledge, having been traditionally carers of natural resources and managers of seeds and

**Fig. 4: A woman taking out paddies from her granary.**

**Fig. 5: A view of a woman winnowing rice.**

medicinal plants. In addition, they are often taking the lead in the defence of indigenous lands and territories and advocating for indigenous peoples' collective rights worldwide. Recognising the women's traditional knowledge in the different stages of production would also reverse the current invisibility of women and promote their status.

**Fig. 6: A view of a girl winnowing paddy grains.**

**Fig. 7: Womenfolk cooking rice at marriage ceremony.**

**Fig. 8: Sticky rice being ground in a wooden mortar by women.**

## References

Brouwers, J.H.A.M. 1993. Rural people's response to soil fertility decline: The Adja case (Benin), Wageningen Agricultural University Papers 93-4.

Census of India. 2011. Manipur District Census Handbook, Ukhrul: Village and Town Wise Primary Census Abstract (PCA). Directorate of Census Operations Manipur. Series-15, Part XII-B.

Fernandez, M.E. 1994. Gender and indigenous knowledge. *Indigenous Knowledge & Development Monitor* 2: 6-7.

Kumar, T.T. 1988. *History of Rice in India: Mythology, Culture, and Agriculture*. New Delhi: Gyan Books.

Marto, J., et al. 2018. Rice water: A traditional ingredient with anti-aging efficacy. *Cosmetics,* 5(26): 1-12. https://www.mdpi.com/2079-9284/5/2/26/htm.

Mosse, D. (1993). Authority, Gender and Knowledge: Theoretical reflections on the practice of participatory rural appraisal. ODI Network Paper 44.

Nene, Y.L. 2005. Rice Research in South Asia through Ages. *Asian Agri-History*, 9(2): 85-106.

Prasad, R. 2012. The Planet Earth, Life, and Agriculture – Science, Mythology, and History. *Asian Agri-History,* 16(2): 111–122.

Posey, D.A. 1995. Indigenous People and Traditional Resource Right: A basis for equitable relationship. Workshop on *the Green College Centre for Environmental Policy & Understanding*. University of Oxford.

Senanayake, S.G.J.N. 2006. Indigenous Knowledge as a key to sustainable development. *Journal of Agricultural Sciences* – Sri Lanka, 2(1), DOI: http://doi.org/10.4038/jas.v2i1.8117.

Smith, M.L. 2006. The Archaeology of Food Preference. *American Anthropologist,* 108(3): 480-493.

Tangvah, K. 2017. Rice Culture and Gender Roles among the Tangkhuls of Ukhrul District, Manipur. Published Ph.D. Thesis, Anthropology Department, NEHU. Shillong.

# 4

# Locusts as Food Source: Examining entomophagy and sustainable practices in north-east India

**Visakhonu Hibo and G. Kanato Chophy**

## Introduction

In 2020, India faced one of the worst attacks of locust swarms in decades. Studies suggested that climate change was the root cause of the desert locust (*Schistocerca gregaria*) swarm that overwhelmed farmlands in northern and northwestern parts of India. In the past, desert locust swarms have been a common occurrence in East Africa and the Arabian Peninsula, which was the outbreak's epicenter, but not on a scale that faced India recently. Not surprisingly, experts had correlated desert locust swarms wreaking havoc in the Horn of Africa, Middle East, and South Asia to climate fluctuations, especially rainfall patterns. Above average monsoon in 2019-20 in the semi-arid regions of East Africa and the Arabian Peninsula was believed to have created favourable conditions for locusts to breed rapidly. The exponential increase of desert locusts was attributed to heavy rain outbursts triggering unusual vegetation growth (with locusts feeding off it) in otherwise arid habitats. This exceptionally long bout of wet weather augmented by rare cyclones that had struck the Eastern African Coast and Arabian Peninsula for many months between 2019–20 was a primary cause. Amid this unusual but recurrent phenomenon, the issue of food insecurity came to the fore.

The United Nations Food and Agricultural Organisation (FAO) reported that India, in 2020, faced the worst outbreak of desert locust swarms in 25 years. The swarm had arrived in India from the spring breeding areas by

May. The entry point was in the Jalore and Jaisalmer districts of Rajasthan on the Indo-Pakistan border, spreading to Banaskantha, Patan, and Mehsana districts in Gujarat. With monsoon around the corner, the locust swarm had spread to states like Andhra Pradesh, Tamil Nadu, Uttar Pradesh, Madhya Pradesh, and Maharashtra, with the center issuing warning to other states like Bihar, Chhattisgarh, and Jharkhand (*The Indian Express,* 2020). The locust swarm had hit India when it was witnessing an outbreak of Covid-19 pandemic, and the exodus of agricultural migrant labourers from the affected areas raised huge concerns about food insecurity. The desert locust swarm posed a massive challenge to agricultural production since, if left unchecked, the insect population is said to increase 20-fold on an average each generation, with the potential to lay vast waste areas of farmlands. The more significant issue lay in the fact that the method of mitigating locusts' swarm posed health and ecological hazards in the long run; this made experts and various stakeholders seek a solution in sustainable practices and traditional knowledge systems of indigenous communities.

## Rethinking Sustainability

There is a profound difference between seeing locusts as a food source or merely as pests. Arguably, this is where the locust-swarm-affected geographic-cultural zone in northern and northwestern India faced a psychological disadvantage – and also lost out on the question of sustainability. Notwithstanding, in the regions with the traditional practice of eating edible insects (entomophagy), health concerns were raised over pesticide use. For example, in Kuwait, high concentrations of residues of organophosphorus pesticides was detected in edible locusts (see Saeed et al. 1993). Pesticides pose a health hazard in East Asia, the Middle East, and South Asia, where locusts are eaten or converted into animal feed. Besides, entomologists are yet to study the impact of climate change on edible insects in many parts of the world. For instance, in Nagaland in north-east India, an entomophagy hub, people have reported an unusual increase in the stink bug population mostly harvested from the riverbed; and most importantly, several cases of food allergy to stink bugs are reported. This phenomenon is not to overemphasize the role of climate change, but environmental changes are possibly altering the metabolism of edible insects.

Food security and sustainable development experts like Arnold Van Huis advocate entomophagy as a viable, alternative food source to meet the challenges of carbon emission and the global food crisis (Huis and Tomberlin, 2017). Recent studies have shown that at least 113 countries practice entomophagy, and an estimated two billion people consume over

2000 documented edible insects worldwide (Tao and Li, 2018). Recent studies have documented about 1900 species of edible insects from tropical zones (Huis et. al 2013). Studies show that the north-east, comprising various ethnic groups, accounts for India's maximum consumption of edible insects. The north-east region has a subtropical climate known for its rich biodiversity.

## Entomophagy in north-east India

Eating edible insects among the tribal communities in north-east India is an age-old tradition. A list of edible insects can give a glimpse of entomophagy among the diverse ethnic communities: among the Karbis of Karbi Anglong district, Assam, Ronghang, and Ahmed (2010) have listed nearly 40 edible insects; a total of 41 edible insects have been identified among the different ethnic communities of Manipur (Shantibala et al. 2012); a study conducted by Meyer-Rochow and Changkija (1997) on the Ao Nagas of Nagaland had identified about 42 edible insect species, and about 102 edible insects have been identified among the tribes of Arunachal Pradesh (Singh et. al 2007).

The practice of eating edible insects is an ecological adaptation that has evolved into a specific cultural knowledge, though not without being frowned upon on the mainland. Researchers have established a relationship between edible insects and the environment, but socio-cultural theorisation remains less explored in the north-east region. For one thing, food has always been political and more so with the protein food source (the controversy over beef eating is a good example). Eating insects is thus not only an ecological adaptation but also has deep roots in cultural beliefs and practices. It will be preposterous to suggest entomophagy to mitigate the desert locusts swarm that can ravage farmlands. However, exploring the viability of melding traditional knowledge with scientific research can throw light on sustainable development.

In India, entomophagy is found among tribal communities. Therefore, it does not come as a surprise that the perception of "primitiveness" is attached to it. Several tribes in India's central, eastern, and western parts consume red ants as a delicacy. However, the variety of edible insects is less among tribes in other parts of India. Culture influences food habits, and the idea of eating insects evokes a feeling of disgust in most societies. Cultural beliefs and values often override meeting the sustainable development goals (meeting protein requirements) even when edible insects like locusts that are part of the local ecosystem jeopardize economic livelihood. Studies show that societies with rice as staple food have an advantage since rice is an ideal vehicle to deliver nutrients from edible insects (Tao and Li, 2018). However, the "yuck" (cultural) factor makes insect protein hitherto undesirable to meet sustainable goals in India.

Generally, eating insects is associated with "primitive" behaviour as the lowest form of food habit (Huis et al. 2013: 35–6). On the contrary, edible insects are considered delicacies (even expensive) and not a primary or emergency food source among the tribes of north-east India. However, there is a changing trend due to globalisation and cultural contact, resulting in the homogenisation of food habits. This condition does not bode well for food security and sustainability in the region since entomophagy is a traditional knowledge system involving livelihood patterns and knowledge about the environment and rarely has to do with "exotic" food habits.

## Cultural perception of locusts

Orthopterans (locusts, grasshoppers, and crickets) are the most resilient insects due to their fast production and adaptive capability. Most notably, orthopterans are commonly known edible insects, with an estimated 80 species of grasshoppers consumed worldwide. Studies among the tribal communities in the north-east show that orthopterans (especially grasshoppers) are the most widely consumed edible insects. For instance, Narzari and Sarmah (2015) identified five grasshopper's species and two cricket's species among the Bodos of Assam. In Arunachal Pradesh, four grasshopper's species, three cricket's species, and one species of edible locusts have been identified among the Nyishi and Galo tribes (Chakravorty et al. 2011).

Orthopterans are found in almost all habitats including tropics, desert lands, temperate grasslands, and rainforests. The association of orthopterans with rice-intensive cultures like the north-east region remains noteworthy. Ethnographic research shows that collecting edible insects is part of agricultural practice to mitigate crop damage. In our study of the Sumi Nagas of Nagaland, farmers attest that grasshopper attack on paddy fields increases the risk of chaffs during harvest; not surprisingly, the Sumi Nagas have developed a taste for grasshoppers consuming them as delicacies. The Apatani of Ziro valley in Arunachal Pradesh, renowned for their sustainable wet rice cultivation, do not have a separate activity for insect collection. However, it is common to see men and women with small bamboo baskets tied around their waists collecting insects as they tend to the rice plants. The practice of entomophagy is inherent to this primary economic livelihood, and edible insects are incorporated into the folk belief, thus establishing cultural significance. Entomophagy is a long-held traditional knowledge that has withstood the test of time. Research shows that insects consumed by tribal communities in the north-east have no sign of adverse health effects (Chakravorty, 2014), barring food allergy to edible insects among some individuals.

When entomophagy is a cultural practice, it is natural for people, like in the north-east, to ask why not resort to eating locusts to control the population, like the one that afflicted northern India. The ground reality is very complex because of the sheer size of the swarm. We are talking about a desert locust swarm that can cover a distance of 130 km in a day, and even a small swarm (1 km square) can consist of about 80 million locusts that can consume the same amount of food as 35,000 people in a day. Notwithstanding that humans have weathered locust swarms in the past: cultural knowledge has played a pivotal role in the adaptation process.

Arguably, the response of traditional knowledge towards the outbreak of locust swarm was found to be lacking on the Indian mainland. The culture adaptability factor still has to develop as an alternative to pesticides, which is not sustainable and can have a detrimental effect in the long run. Researchers need to identify and document sustainable practices from diverse communities in India to combat locust swarms that are here to stay as climate change becomes inevitable. The easily replicable knowledge may include techniques for trapping locusts and finding economic incentives for mass harvesting (one of our Naga respondents suggested pickling locusts for a commercial purpose).

Among the tribal communities in north-east India, the practice of eating insects is a form of cultural adaptation. For instance, the Naga tribes settled in the plains of Dimapur district, Nagaland, practicing wet rice cultivation, had to face the menace of rice grasshoppers (*Heiroglyphus banian*) and crickets (*Meloimorpha cincticornis*). Thus, entomophagy for them is a cultural complex, as it is interconnected with the agricultural rhythms, material culture, and knowledge about insects. Without intervention, the farmers know that grasshoppers can multiply rapidly, causing irreparable damage to the rice plants. So one of the effective ways is resorting to mass harvesting of grasshoppers. Eating grasshoppers has twice the benefit, as it mitigates the grasshopper population and is also a delicacy. To reduce grasshopper populations, the farmers have devised easily replicable techniques like lighting the compact fluorescent lamp (CFL) nearby paddy fields to attract grasshoppers and using mosquito nets to trap them.

Besides, the Nagas do not use pesticides to control the population of rice grasshoppers and crickets. The human agency remains a decisive factor since, given the incentive, humans can overwhelm the grasshopper population, as is demonstrable among the Nagas in Dimapur. Locusts and grasshoppers are a delicacy and are sold in the local markets. Therefore, during a particular time of the agricultural year, it is common to see hundreds of people with torches thronging the rice fields to catch grasshoppers in the nighttime. This activity seems to be a case where the cultural practice of eating edible insects proves helpful for economic livelihood.

## Conclusion

Entomophagy among the tribal communities in north-east India existed long before the pesticides were patented. It will continue to be practiced, though the fast track to modernity has tremendously affected the traditional knowledge system of the tribes. The Indian welfare state in this region remains noticeable, but policymaking should consider the region's cultural and ecological parameters. For instance, farmers in Dimapur narrate their experience that high-yielding variety rice introduced by government agencies is more prone to insect attack like grasshoppers. Also, the central government has approved a list of pesticides like chlorpyrifos, deltamethrin, fipronil, and malathion to be used on crops and trees to control the desert locust outbreak.

The tribal communities in the north-east are rendered more vulnerable because of rapid environmental changes and the indiscriminate use of pesticides. Therefore, policymakers need to consider whether traditional knowledge systems can mitigate the outbreak of locust swarms in the north-east. They need to take communities into confidence before implementing policies like introducing pesticides at par with other geographic-cultural zones in the country since north-east India as a region has its unique set of challenges and advantages. Besides, concerning India's Act East Policy, the north-east is untapped in food tourism potential, and the diverse knowledge on edible insects can be icing on the cake, but it should not come with a dash of pesticides.

## Acknowledgment

The authors thank the University Grants Commission (UGC) for funding the research. The data were collected as part of UGC-STRIDE research project on "Naga indigenous cuisines, agrobiodiversity, climate change, and food security."

## References

Chakravorty, Jharna (2014): "Diversity of Edible Insects and Practices of Entomophagy in India: An Overview," *Biodiversity, Bioprospecting and Development*, Vol. 1, Issue 3.

Chakravorty, J., S. Ghosh and V.B. Meyer-Rochow (2011): "Practices of Entomophagy and Entomotherapy by Members of the Nyishi and Galo Tribes, two Ethnic Groups of the State of Arunachal Pradesh (North-East India)," *Journal of Ethnobiology and Ethnomedicine*, Vol. 7, Issue 5.

Huis, Arnold van et. al (2013): "*Edible Insects: Future Prospects for Food and Feed Security*," Rome: Food and Agriculture Organisation of the United Nations.

Huis, Arnold van and Jeffery K. Tomberlin (eds) (2017): "*Insects as Food and Feed: From Production to Consumption*," Wageningen: Wageningen Academic Publishers.

Meyer-Rochow, V.B. and S. Changkija (1997): "Uses of Insects as Human Food in Papua New Guinea, Australia and North-East India: Cross-cultural Considerations and Cautious Conclusions," *Ecology of Food and Nutrition*, Vol. 36, pp. 159–185.

Narzari, Silistina and Jatin Sarmah (2015): "A Study on the Prevalence of Entomophagy among the Bodos of Assam," *Journal of Entomology and Zoology Studies*, Vol. 3, No. 2, pp. 315–320.

Ronghang, R. and R. Ahmed (2010): "Edible Insects and their Conservation Strategy in Karbi Anglong District of Assam, North East India," *Bioscan,* Vol. 2, pp. 515–521.

Saeed, T., F.A. Dagga and M. Saraf (1993): "Analysis of Residual Pesticides Present in Edible Locusts Captured in Kuwait," *Arab Journal of Scientific Research*, Vol. 11, No. 1 pp. 1–5.

Shantibala, T, R.K. Lokeshwari and H.D. Sharma (2012): Entomophagy Practices among the Ethnic Communities of Manipur, North East India," *IJIIT,* Vol. 5, pp. 13–20.

Singh, O.T., J. Chakravorty, S. Nabam and D. Kato (2007): "Species Diversity and Occurrence of Edible Insects with Special Reference to Coleopterans of Arunachal Pradesh," *Journal of Nature Conservation*, Vol. 19, No. 1, pp. 159–66.

Tao, Jaynie and Yao Olive Li (2018): "Edible Insects as a Means to Address Global Malnutrition and Food Insecurity Issues," *Food Quality and Safety*, Vol. 2, pp. 17–26.

*The Indian Express* (2020): "Locust Attack Tracker: New States where the Insects are Headed," 2 June, https://indianexpress.com/article/india/locust-attack-tracker-rajasthan-maharashtra-uttar-pradesh-gujarat-tamil-nadu-andhra-pradesh-karnataka-6435962/.

# 5

# Religious Environmental Philosophies and The Question of Sustainability – A Study Among the Pnar of Nangbah

**Clarissa Candace Giri**

## Abstract

The origins of the Khasi and their religious philosophies largely revolve around nature, emerged from animistic roots and is the bond that binds the people to their land. The following paper was derived as part of the ethnographic fieldwork for the degree of Doctor of Philosophy in Anthropology, from a study conducted among the *Pnar*, a subset of the larger Khasi Tribe also called the *Hynñiew Trep* people, of Nangbah, West Jaiñtia Hills, Meghalaya. The paper discusses the *Ñiam Tre* religious philosophies around nature and environment of the people of Nangbah through the various religious rites performed, tries to delineate the extent and impact of modernity and globalisation on indigenous practices and discusses a need for environmental awareness among the people with regard to sustainability in their ritual practices through a structure based functional approach, a symbolic-interaction approach which ensued mostly through the observation method, both non-participant and participant including interviews and conversations.

**Keywords:** environment, ecology, sustainability, religion, philosophy, rituals, modernity, globalisation.

## Introduction

The late Soso Tham accentuates that to the Khasis', the environment is a library essentially because Khasi culture largely revolves around nature, from ritual practices, to oral traditions in stories of origin, folktales and folklore, in their lifestyle and identity. The Khasi consists of the Khynriam, the Pnar or Synteng or Jaiñtia, the Bhoi, the War and the Lyngngam as per Lyngdoh (1937); Mawrie, (2014). Notwithstanding, originally from the olden days, only one type of people settled in this area known as the Khasis. The Jaiñtias or Pnars as we call them today are only a name invented by the British in pursuit of their policy of 'divide and rule.' They both share common oral traditions and beliefs. This paper gives insight into some of the references made to the natural environment in the rituals and beliefs of the Khasi, with special reference towards the Pnar people of Meghalaya, specifically from Nangbah, West Jaiñtia Hills.

The oral traditions of the origin of all Khasi subtribes speak of the descent of celestial beings to begin the human race on Earth. In Khynriam dialect the term *Hynñiewtrep* or Seven Huts is used to denote descents that came down to Earth to form the human race. They were part of the sixteen huts of which nine stayed behind in heaven. While in the Pnar story of origin they call the sixteen huts as *Khadhynru Wasa.* According to Lamare (2013), *U Tre Kirot* or God had ordered the *Niaw Wasa* or Seven Huts to go down to a special place for preparation, i.e., the Earth. The main reason they came down to earth was at the persistent plead of mother nature to God to send some celestials from the sixteen huts to look after her land, to work, till it, make it fit for agriculture for livelihood and to take care of and to live in harmony with all other creatures on earth. The present paper was derived from a study conducted among the *Pnar* (a subset of the larger Khasi Tribe also called the *Hynñiew Trep* people) of Nangbah, West Jaiñtia Hills, Meghalaya, as part of a larger ethnographic fieldwork for the degree of Doctor of Philosophy in Anthropology.

The paper discusses the *Ñiam Tre* religious philosophies around nature and environment, with special focus on the people of Nangbah, through the various religious rites performed by them. The paper also addresses remnants of rapid modernity and globalisation and attempts to delineate the extent and impact of improper assimilation and adaptation on the lives of the people, their beliefs and the changes caused by it; furthermore, discussing the need for environmental awareness among the people with regard to sustainability in their ritual practices.

## Research area and Methodology

The study area is a village located in Thadlaskeiñ block, West Jaiñtia Hills, Meghalaya. The people of the village call it *Nangbah* some sign boards that stand on its borders to show the same, yet according to google maps and government details, the name of the village is spelt *Nongbah*, for convenience, uniformity and ease of comprehension, the village will be referred to as Nangbah as per what the villagers like to call it. The people of Nangbah may be classified into two broad categories; the Christians and the Ñiam Tre. Within the village, the area was prominently divided into the *Skur* or Christian dominated areas and the *Chnong* for the Ñiam Tre dominated areas. The arrival of Christianity and the touch of time has brought big shifts in the way people live life in the village. Considering that, the approaches taken for this study such as a structure based functional approach, a symbolic-interaction approach ensued mostly through the observation method, both non-participant and participant including formal interviews and informal conversations in tandem with secondary resource analysis. The study gives insight into change and continuity and on where the Khasi-Pnar people stand today in relation to the ancient promises made between humans and their environment when the very first humans initially arrived on earth.

## Ñiam Tre Religious Philosophies Around Nature and Environment of the People of Nangbah

For the Khasi, there is only one God that is the most prioritised detail in the traditional folk religion. It can be understood that God is envisioned as one who is without and at the same time, with many genders and forms; a multidimensional being of whom nature- *Ka Ramew*[1], is an integral part of; this, therefore makes nature God as well. At the very onset, nature plays a role in the creation of humans, after the plea made by mother nature or *"Ka Mei Ramew"*. The descent of the celestial Seven huts was made possible through a gateway *U Dieingïei*[2], the first tree and doorway between heaven and Earth. The great tree was perched on the topmost point of *U Lum Diengiei*[3]. It was also believed that the first humans descended and ascended from the navel of heaven called *U Sohpetbneng*. It is uncertain to locate the gateway, or if both descriptions are a varied form of one gateway. However, either way *U Lum Sohpet Bneng*[4] is a place of pilgrimage and ritual practice for every Khasi even today, especially for those who still follow the traditional folk religion. This is the very beginning of the religious Khasi philosophy that highlights a strong connection between them and their environment; the concepts and principles of Khasi folklore represent a cultural belief system that reflects the most cherished wisdom of the world's perennial philosophy (Malngiang, 1991).

Among the Ñiam Tre population of Nangbah, it is believed that the life of human beings on Earth began with *Ka Lei Synshar,* Goddess of rule and governance, who first placed humankind on earth in a state of holiness and innocence. She is also the highest goddess in Pnar mythology. Thus, to return to innocence humans can atone and be made holy again through the various rites and rituals that exist in the religion, given to them by God. It is believed that when the humans first settled on earth, they had to build settlements, and the son of Ka Lei Synshar, *U Syiem Pyrthat*[5] was sent by *U Blei*[6] to break *Musiangtari* or *Musiang*[7] (which are the great boulders, foundations of the earth, also another name for Mother Earth), the Sun and the Moon, believed to be the children of *Ka Musiang,* wept bitterly and protested to the killing of their mother but U Blei promised them that she won't die yet live on in various forms such as the various stones used in Khasi culture such as *mawpun, mawpud, mawshan, marai*[8] *(maw buh shyieng in khasi), mawbynna etc.*

From the rocks and boulders that make the ground firm, to the very soil itself, each aspect of nature has a life of its own, a past and an ancient history according to mythology. The Goddesses *Synshar, Iawbei* and *Lukhmi*, were said to have carried the soil and debris and formed the lands and caves and rivers and waterfalls and from that time the soil was fit for planting and the herbs flourished (Laloo, 2000). Since the ones who first vouched for the humans were the plants and all the flora in nature, they formed a binding covenant for all time with humans which is why the Khasi are very much knowledgeable about and reliant on their traditional healing and herbal medicine.

The rituals in Nangbah are classified into different types, those for the household, for the clan and for the village as a whole. The rites are performed on the basis of three basic principles- for the welfare of being human, for agricultural wellness and prosperity, and for good fortune in the affairs of business and trade. It is peculiar to note that for every season, a ritual is performed for the season and the reigning deities of each season. A ritual is performed for *U Syiem Pyrthat Syiem Iaiong Iangiat*, it is to be noted that this is the king of lightning and storms another type of seasonal ritual is the *Ñiam Khie Liyur* at the peak of Summer. The Pnar people have a way of calculating the days, weeks, months and seasons according to their own Almanak. The new year begins on the first day of the *Kñia Lyngdoh* ritual for agricultural prosperity, which begins with the *Sam Klong* an event that takes place inside the stone garden called *Iawmusiang*[9], a passing around of the klong or libation gourd among all representations of each clan inside a megalith garden headed by the *U Lyngdoh* and *U Daloi* of Nangbah, this is symbolic and yet a meeting to collect offering from each clan for the celebrations that await in the days to come. The women go round offering *Kwai*[10] and betel leaves, a symbol of camaraderie and unity among the clans.

During the main ritual in the *Kñia Lyngdoh* festival, the men from every clan go to the sacred forest to sacrifice a multitude of chickens offered by the many people of the village. But the women must stay behind, no woman is allowed to enter the grove when the Gods are invoked. This ritual takes place in the month of April when sowing begins. This time is the prime of spring when the heavy rains begin in Meghalaya accompanied with thunderstorms and strong winds. It is believed that rain must fall at the end of the sacrifice as a sign that the gods have accepted the sacrifices and have sent the rain to wash away all the blood symbolising that all the sins and errors of humankind have been washed away too.

When this festival was observed in April 2021, it so happened that a huge thunderstorm hit the village and neighbouring areas right after the ritual sacrifice of chickens ended. The storm lasted, with what seemed an unyielding ferocity, for about four hours. It was later revealed, in conversation with a clan elder - the secretary of the *Seiñ Raij*[11] of Nangbah, that such fierceness in a storm after a *Kñia Lyngdoh* sacrifice usually never took place the way it did earlier that day; even when the rains are expected and looked forward to after the ritual was performed in the sacred grove, the rains came to cleanse and did not fall in 'anger'. The violent showers were a sign that the gods were very angry and dissatisfied, to the point that the elder had to talk to them during the onslaught of rain and wind, to calm the gods down so that the remaining part of the festival could be completed. The clan elder here, also mentioned that he needed to converse with them later in the week, so that the reasons that have invoked so much wrath from the gods could be revealed and be made known in order to allow the people to expiate with the necessary rituals.

Nature plays a most important role, revered and respected by way of religion… Religion is neither a human affair alone nor their monopoly… but nature takes part in their religious practices in a very tangible and respectable manner. Her presence is invoked and solicited and human beings surround her with due reverence (Mawrie, 2009).

The Khasi do not worship in churches or temples nor in specific architectural spaces made for sacrifices. Instead, nature is the altar and the sanctuary for any sacrifice (Mawrie, 2009). There exists a deep relationship and connection between human beings and nature. In any Khasi sacrifice we see the intimacy which the Khasi have with nature, especially in the things they use for sacrifice (Mawrie, 2009). In every ritual sacrifice, also witnessed among the Pnar of Nangbah, the death of the sacrificial animal is considered a consecrated and most honourable form of death. Because of the ancient covenant between *U Syiar*[12] and the Goddess *Synshar* when there was only darkness on earth brought about by the disappearance of the Sun, the egg *Ka Pylleng* a poor and naked being was transformed, cracked and opened to become U Syiar, with all its glorious colours, clad in red, orange, yellow and gold (Colours of wealth in Khasi culture).This is to bring back the light to create a path for beings to follow not get lost in the darkness. But for that the Cock will bear the burden on its neck. Thus, the sacrifice made of chickens is done accordingly especially in death rites. A cock is sacrificed to create a path for the deceased to cross over into the ancestral realm to be able to eat *Kwai* at God's house. The egg is the witness to this covenant, by death and is used in divination, in ceremonies such as *Ka Pam Mynso* and *Noh Mynso* after the birth of a child. Thereby, bad omens and evil spirits are removed, as a witness to the cleansing of the rot of a dead body by fire. While, the egg is thrown onto a great tree by the cremation site to bear witness to the adequacy of the pyre for burning the deceased etc.

Some games are also played as part of the *Kñia Lyngdoh* festival, by men from every clan in Iawmusiang, the Megalith market. Anybody can try to lift and carry a round boulder three to four times the size of a football over their head. Those who succeed will ensure that their crop will be the best that year and those who fail to lift the boulder will face troublesome yield. In this show of strength, one is compelled to reflect to the ancient stories of *Ka Musiangtari* who was broken up by U Syiem Pyrthat and carried by the goddesses to make the soil, the sand, rivers and waterfalls and enabled the land to be tilled and fit for planting and for thriving of herbs. Symbolically, this ritual game represents the ancient covenant that serves as a reminder human responsibility towards mother nature and the land given. Hence, in the religious philosophy of the Khasi, the Pnar in this context, human beings were allowed to live on earth by nature, vouched for by nature, provided for by nature, and their bodies will be returned to nature just as their souls return to God. According to these tenets, their life on earth must be to earn their righteousness, to know who their clan members are and who their father's clan members are, and to be aware of and respect other beings and above all- God (meaning the very environment they live in).

## The Impact of Globalisation: with special focus on packaged food items

Globalisation presents a picture of westernisation, a clash between the western and the non-western civilisations and between non-western civilisations (Pieterse, 2009). A leaching of cultural heritage, access to and the trying on of global drifts in fashion, technology, language, culture and the packages that come with them, all spell out globalisation. The main idea of which is to be up to speed with the times, to familiarise oneself with the culture trends propagated through social media platforms such as YouTube, Instagram, Twitter and countless more. Going further back in time before the bombardment of the internet, the first prominent defining trait of globalisation's touch is the packaged food market. While many other items sold include a wide array of non-edible commodities, we look at the edible commodities in this paper because food plays an important role in the rituals of the people and their environment.

In Sunday school, we were taught that missionaries, with their good intent, brought the West into the Khasi Hills, which slowly spread all over, which included the Jaiñtia Hills. It would have been very intriguing, especially to a small tribe in the hills in a small corner of the country. Healthcare was the main attraction for indigenous people, the first stepping stone into conversion to Christianity. The next step was food and nutrition that was provided to the people who were made to believe they were needy. Because they were not from the "West" and the 'generosity' of the foreign mission placed the missionaries in everyone's good graces. This made the food that came in packages look and feel exotic and rare; with time, as more trade and business influx began to pick up, packaged food items became fun food for children, somewhere along the line. Eventually, packed food items have become gifts and snacks for children, and Nangbah is no exception. The after-school affairs for children and their guardians always include a quick stop at the various local 'knick-knack' shops for chips, sweets, soft-drinks and other beguiling eccentricities.

The most interesting observation however, were the baskets of offerings filled with all these goodies as well; inside the aged bamboo baskets, food offerings were made of packaged *daal chana.* Sometimes a popular Indian snack called *Rompom* (instant pre-cooked noodles), not to leave out juice boxes, cream biscuits, fried *Fryums* in tiny plastic casings, bottled commercial liquor in plastic water bottles and many more processed foods along with a touch of the traditional such as rice breads. Palm oil has stealthily made its way into the religious practices of the people as well, through packaged food materials in chips, biscuits and noodles, replacing the symbolic and statutory significance of traditional food. Traditional food is often sneered at by children who are the ones who actually benefit the most from it; instead they do not refuse processed food items which may in turn, later have detrimental effects on their growing bodies and brains that have been for generations nutritionally met with indigenous food.

In every ritual, a certain amount of waste is generated, organic waste, from leftovers of sacrificial offerings like eggshells from eggs used in divination, to charred and half burnt wood left behind from funeral pyres. Nature provides and takes away, evident too in the people's concept of cremation; notably, cremation takes place in the open air with an ancient tree around to bear witness to the act of cremation. Interestingly, a crematorium has been constructed for the people, to conserve natural resources; however, the people rarely used the crematorium because they believe that it will upset nature and the ancestors and if used, more people will die. The onus lies upon the leaders and educated sections of society to help make people aware and understand the purpose of new technology. The general process follows that is, the burnt wood and partially burnt wood are thrown back to nature, similarly with all sacrificial waste from the various sacrificial offerings, food items included, therefore this practice of the people to use and throw whatever is left behind, back into nature's bosom to succumb to time comes naturally to them and everything the people used was biodegradable and sustainable.

However, when packaged food items come into play. As a result, a trail of waste (non-biodegradable waste) gets left behind, resulting in numerous waste heaps found at certain spots and intervals all around the village. These remnants of globalisation are found amidst sacred places along with the ash heap of burnt burial wood, there would be waste that do not decompose such as plastic bottles, vessels that held oil used to cleanse the bones to make worthy for burial, and other food packets lay in wait for an end that will never come while the trees bare witness.

## Conclusion

From the above findings and observations, one can say that the paradox that exists is that the large-scale littering, improper waste disposal and management in the village is both not solely the fault of the people and yet it is also the responsibility of every person in the village. Modernisation has been advancing like a steamroller, erasing cultural and biological diversity in its way, and… Stamping out cultural diversity has been a form of disenchantment of the world (Pieterse, 2009). The rude awakening to the down side of globalisation is the flood of illusions about development and modernity that has been imposed on a people from an arbitrary place of power beyond the cultural reach of their society. Development must occur according to the cultural ethics and understanding of a society. It must be allowed to grow from the people within, not come from a place that is ignorant of the mechanics of the culture it impacts. But that kind of Utopia does not exist and cannot exist anymore. However, people can be made aware of the negative impacts and with awareness new perspectives can be awakened.

People must always have the option to be made aware of the environmental impacts of improper waste disposal, the negative effects they can have on the air quality, their soil, their water bodies and how to achieve sustainability through their pre-existing traditional knowledge. Though globalisation has allowed individuals to access the world through tiny black screens, the detachment from nature and each other is still a threat and poses an urgent requirement to revive the practice of oral traditions. There is a question that has become apparent about the need to remind the people of their cultural background; from the study conducted at Nangbah, an observation can be made, that also applies to the many who diligently follow age-old teachings, that what elders and religious leaders reinforce in people holds significance in how the people see the world and shapes their thought process as well. One such example can be extracted from interviews with women, during the *Kñia Lyngdoh* festival; when asked why women were not allowed to enter the grove, the response was inconclusive and firm, that ultimately because they have never done that, they believe that it is taboo and the gods will be displeased. Therefore, the majority of the people themselves possess limited knowledge as to why the rituals are performed and what significance these rituals possess towards them individually, as a community and in their environment. This poses a threat to the survival of indigenous knowledge and the wholeness of the culture itself.

The more optimistic side to these findings is that culture adapts and will always find a way to persevere with its dynamic nature; also, on the other hand, Environmental Awareness Programmes have been set up in the village and are ongoing. With additional revitalisation programmes to help inculcate a better understanding of the religious relationship between the belief system and their environment, it would tremendously contribute to allow the people to become more aware of their surroundings, and be able to take care of their environment better. Furthermore, an added initiative to bring understanding of how beliefs and scientific facts around conservation and sustainability are connected, would benefit the people and their future generations on a large scale. This study does not condemn the people and place whereby the research was conducted, however it was sampled to reflect on the dilemma we all face as human beings and as a community; and that we too need to be reminded of ancient covenants made through folktales and folk narratives, to learn and develop a more nature-oriented mindset that can help shape a better future for the generations to come, so that they too can carry their culture and religious environmental philosophies forward.

## References

Laloo, Donbok. T. (2000). *U Syiar*. Scorpio Printers Mawkhar.

Lamare, Sobhan N. (2013). *The Jaintias: Studies in Society and Change.* Regency Publications Adivision of Astral International Pvt. Ltd.

Lyngdoh, Homiwell. (1937). *Ka Ñiam Khasi.* Ri Khasi Press.

Malngiang, Pascal. (1991). *Aspects of Khasi Philosophy*. Seven Huts Enterprise.

Mawrie, Barnes L. (2014). *Khasi Ethics.* Vendrame Institute Publications.

Mawrie, Barnes L. (2009). *The Khasis and their Natural Environment: A Study of the Eco-Consciousness and Eco-Spirituality of the Khasis.* Vendrame Institute Publications.

Passah, P.M. & S. Sarma. (2002). *Jaintia Hills- A Meghalaya Tribe, Its Environment, Land and People.* Reliance Publishing House.

Pieterse, Jan Nederveen. (2009). *Globalisation and Culture: Global Mélange*. Rowman and Littlefield Publishers, Inc.

# 6

# Interrelatedness between Tribal Spirituality and Sustainability; a Literature review concerning the Oraons in Jharkhand

**Hemant Tigga, & Dr T. Neishoning Koireng**

**Abstract**

It is important to explore the connection between spirituality and sustainability because this seems to be a viable approach that might save our environment. Our Environment is going through a crisis and we are responsible for it because of our faulty habits. Tribal traditions have offered excellent examples of living sustainably without jeopardizing the ecological equilibrium. They might be living examples of practicing sustainability while living spiritually.

Oraons are animists known for sustainable living. The paper explores the spiritual life and worldview of Oraons through a literature review. It seeks the lessons of sustainability in the cultural actions of Oraons, which is intrinsically rooted in their spirituality. It is a contemplation on whether living a spiritual life makes our practices more sustainable; and can we infer that the solution to the Global problem of sustainability can be learned from the indigenous tribe like Oraons? And is there a relation between tribal spirituality and sustainability?

**Keywords:** Oraons, Tribal spirituality, Sustainability, Oraons in Jharkhand, Tribals.

## Introduction

We have seen nature as a resource for fulfilling our insatiable and endless demands. In our greed, we thought we are free to use it as much as we want. We have never seen it in its totality but as a means for meeting our ends. We have seen it as a separate entity from us, which is there just for fulfilling our needs. These habits and perceptions have greatly harmed nature; therefore, we need to reconsider and redefine our relationship with nature and this requires a holistic sustainability movement.

The Oraons are one of South Asia's five biggest tribes. They dwell in the wooded uplands of east-central India, mostly in Jharkhand's Chota Nagpur area and surrounding states. Traditionally, Oraons drew their ceremonial and economic sustenance from the forest and farmland, but in recent years, a small number of them have settled down as mostly agriculturalists. For India's reservation system, they are considered a Scheduled Tribe. Oraons are Kurukh speakers who belong to the Dravidian family's northern branch. The Oraon adore nature and practice their ancient religion (Sarnaism).

In this paper, we are seeking the solution to the Global problem of sustainability in the spiritual life of the Oraon tribe. We are exploring the cultural practice of Oraons through literature review and diving deeper into their spiritual life interwoven with their culture for sustainability lessons. We are establishing the interrelatedness between tribal spirituality and sustainability through the unique worldview of Oraons.

## Spirituality

There can be many definitions of spirituality because it is a subjective concept. The definition could vary with people and the author. However, it is important to understand that any attempt to categorise it as an idea will objectify it, since it is subjective, it should not be categorised. In a broader sense, spirituality is more of a practice and should be reflected in action than an idea or concept (Neal, 1997).

Its value lies in imbibing the concept in daily life practice, in thought process, in decision making. It must be an active force in your subconscious and should be capable of changing your behaviour pattern. It is not a superficial ritual. Spirituality talks about genuine heartfelt concern and support for others, fairly treating others, behaving with compassion, kindness, empathy, actively attending to the needs of others, justice, and fairness in the decision making. Above all, it should be done irrespective of the class and place of the person in the power structure.

It is not a new concept but a much-required one. It can minimize differences in society by bringing equality and harmony. It insists that change should be inside-out, and then only it can be permanent. They live with the natural sensitiveness for all these kingdoms and consciously engage themselves in maintaining and uplifting them.

## Sustainability

The concept of Sustainable development has been first defined as "development that meets the needs of the present without compromising the ability of the future generations to meet their own needs" (The report 'Our common future' of the Brundtland Commission, 1987). Ever since the emergence of this concept, it has drawn the attention of the world towards the much-ignored issues of ill effects of globalisation, changing biodiversity, and questioning the survival of the coming generations (Giddings et al., 2002).

It challenged the existing model of development which brought ozone depletion, forest depletion, soil degradation, extinction of species, global warming, and disturbing ecological balance of the mother earth. It has revealed the short-sightedness and unawareness with which these development processes were implemented. It brought change, now the concept of development was also analyzed from the environmental aspects, along with social, economic, and political aspects. It has made us know that there is an urgent need to shift the awareness of humans how they see the world.

## Interrelatedness between Spirituality and Sustainability

For a holistic sustainability movement, we need to create a society that is sensitive and responsible, in this regard people who are spiritual and actively working on expanding their consciousness can play an important role (Gupta, et al., 2016).

Certainly, it won't be unjust to say that our spiritual alienation and the global spread of materialism have destroyed the natural world. The western origin of science and technology has failed to value the sacred which has found its manifestation in the earth through nature. A collective spiritual crisis has made us encourage bad engineering which consequently disrupted the ecological balance (Berry, 1979).

We were given no choice but to accept developmental models which were against our traditional environmental wisdom. The bulldozer of globalisation has overshadowed the traditional philosophies of protecting nature; it was made to look old and anti-development in front of the new-economic order imposed by the west. We have allowed traditional wisdom to be manipulated for the validation and justification of the environmental damages.

## Interrelatedness between Spirituality and Religion

Spirituality is a universal concept that encompasses culture, gender, religious background, and personal experience (Dhiman & Marques, 2016). Spirituality heals people and the environment. They often support simple living, opposing the attitude of exploitation that pervades consumer society and is rooted in greed. Today's environmental assaults are the result of population, wealth, and hazardous technologies. At its best, the world's religions call into question affluent indulgences (McDonald, 2018).

However, many ancient religious traditions fail to emphasize a sense of kinship with creation, which is also essential for sustainable life, even in their core teachings. Some of these faiths, particularly those that are text-based rather than nature-based, exaggerate human-divine; and human-human relationships at the price of highlighting human interconnectedness in a greater web of life. The good news is that religions, like science, evolve, and their inherited fundamentals are not final. More Earth-conscious teachings can be embraced by religions. Even a religion's essence is a work-in-progress, susceptible to fresh adaptation to new circumstances. Sustainability necessitates such adaptability in religion.

## Tribal spirituality

Tribal traditions have always offered great examples of living sustainably without harming the ecological balance. Their practice of worshiping trees and considering animals as holy has paved the path of sustainability from the lenses of spirituality (Kala and Sharma, 2010). The integration of spirituality is adequately reflected in tribal life; it has given them deep ecological concern. They value nature for its inherent worth and perceive nature as an identical entity to humans, holistic growth of the community (Devall and Sessions, 1985).

They have developed a tolerance for diversity and adopted decentralised, non-hierarchical governance, the self-regulating structure of society, small-scale, and community-based economic models. They have simplicity in their wants and needs and they don't exhaust nature because their demands are not insatiable.

The land is life; there is no life without land, say indigenous peoples all across the world. This is part of the indigenous people's overall life philosophy. Indigenous peoples of Orissa, Chhattisgarh, Jharkhand, and other areas of India are recognised and supported by those who envision an ecological democracy for long-term development (Shrivastava & Kothari, 2012). The writers argued unambiguously that Indigenous peoples across the world have typically lived by an innate sense of ecological integrity; because they have kept true to their origin in their search for a new model of development.

## Method

The literature search is done through several internet searches in the search engines like Google Scholar, Research gate, Sci-hub, CUJ E-library, etc. From a record of a thousand articles, the authors of this paper reviewed more than fifty articles. The quantitative articles fitting the topic were selected using the combination of keywords, Oraons, Tribal spirituality, Sustainability, Oraons in Jharkhand, Tribals, etc. Then, the articles were critically reviewed multiple times by both authors one after another.

## Findings: The spiritual life of Oraons and Sustainability

Reliance on the Holy Spirit, devotion to justice, community-centeredness, dependency on land, forest, and water, anti-greed attitude, human-nature-spirit continuum, equality between men and women; and so on are some of the significant elements that can be recognised in Oraon's spirituality. Their spirituality is inextricably linked to life and everything it entails, including freedom and nourishment, dignity and equality, community and resource sharing, creativity, and worship of the God of life and liberation (Gnanadason, 1991).

In Oraons, a person is defined in terms of the group to which he or she belongs. The family, lineage, clan, and tribe all contribute to this sense of belonging. Oraons consider their family to include not only their father, mother, children, and grandchildren; but also their brothers and sisters, their wives and children, their nephews and nieces, and anybody else descended from a common ancestor (Isizoh, 1998).

They draw energy and inspiration from their cosmic religiousness in their battles and protests against capitalism and imperialism's anti-cosmic/anti-human forces. This sort of spirituality would involve care for the earth and its resources as needed, rather than otherworldliness, which prevents or tends to inhibit the emergence of a socially engaged spirituality. It has global implications, requiring all people to share land and its resources.

The relations extend beyond a nuclear family; a person is complete only in so far as they are part of the community. In Oraon society, there is no individual life as such. For example, there are no individual dances. All their songs and dances are meant for common singing. As for the authority of the songs and dances too, there are generally no individual authors-nobody knows how many songs and dances have come into being. Community authorship behind the Oraon songs and dances may be deduced. In addition, Oraons live, work, suffer and die in solidarity with one another. Sick in the family and the village are taken care of, needy are helped, agricultural activities are accomplished jointly.

## The holistic view of life

Respect for people, animals, birds, trees, and fish, as well as relation to/respect for ancestors, current ones, and those yet to be born, in the past, present, and future, is implied by a holistic view of existence. The concepts of space and time are thought to be mutually inclusive. The spirituality of Oraons gives significance to creation as a dynamic and deeply interwoven Web of Life (Ekka, 2011).

It oozes life-giving ideas like land sanctity, reverence for all species, wise use, conservation of the earth's resources, and compassion for the weak, oppressed, and disenfranchised. Many people regard these cosmic values, rites, and activities as superstitious. But they capture a cosmic interwovenness that can become a healing and transforming experience for people all over the world.

The Oraons perspective on life's wholeness is expressed and lived in a variety of ways. Humans, according to this concept, share life with rocks, plants, birds, and animals, which coexist rather than exist in isolation. All that is human is built based on the planet. As a result, the ground is sacred, it serves as the central point of reference, and all religious activities revolve around it (Longcaer, 2010).

The land is held in great respect in Oraon communities, and it is controlled and handed out according to people's needs, such as the number of children they have. It is redistributed rather than inherited individually, and hence is not considered private property. From the beginning of time, the earth's Oraons have maintained this vision for humanity: life in all of its richness, in balance and harmony. Oraon spirituality offers a pluralistic, life-centered, and land-centered understanding of reality, in which reality is experienced as interconnected and interrelated.

The spiritual dimension of a person has a significant impact on their sense of self, basic attitude toward life, ethos, and worldview, all of which influence behavioural form as well as the kind and quality of the culture they practice. The culture was developed by humans, but since it was created by the Supreme Being, it is only natural that it would include spirituality (Lakra, 2005).

The Oraons have no concept of sacred and secular, even though they do not have a term to explain spirituality precisely. Spirituality is not a separate entity for them; it is intertwined with their entire religion-socio-cultural lives. Spirituality, for Oraons, entails a human yearning and effort to make contact with the Divine, as well as an attempt to live a more human honest life. That only is the central aspect of Oraon's spirituality.

## Relation to Creation

Concerning creation, thanks to the Creator, non-transferability, and non-possessiveness of the earth (land) are all rooted in the concept that everything comes from God and is hence sacred and worthy of special respect (Kullu, 1996). The idea that everything has its origin in and from Dharmesh is reflected in Oraons' respect for creation, thankfulness to the Creator, non-transferability, and non-possessiveness of the land. As a result, it is sacrosanct and deserving of special attention. They believe in collective land ownership. They follow the natural cycle of life.

## Conclusions

To recapitulate, the connections between spirituality and sustainability are easing the path to knowledge and a healthy society in every way. Which actions must be taken to minimize and eradicate environmental damage? Spirituality is inextricably related to humanity. Spirituality is significant at both the local and macro levels. It alters people's behaviour and pushes them to be more open with their peers (Matlock & Jurin, 2016). Spirituality increases people's awareness and observance of their inner and outer worlds in general. It makes a significant contribution toward modifying what is required. Spiritual people are more sensitive and eager to make significant and constructive changes to see the environment as a reflection of them.

Interrelatedness between spirituality and sustainability can be observed in Oraon's collective land ownership, intertwined religion-socio-cultural lives, cosmic interwovenness, community ownership of creative works, solidarity with one another, socially engaged spirituality, cosmic religiousness, innate sense of ecological integrity, tolerance for diversity, decentralised, and non-hierarchical governance, and their practices of not exhausting nature by rationally checking their demands to keep it minimum.

## References

Gupta, K., Agarwal, R., & Sharma, V. (2016). *Sustainability from the lenses of spirituality: a new perspective.*

Neal, J. A. (1997). *Spirituality in Management Education: A Guide to Resources.*

Giddings, B., Hopwood, B. & O'Brien, G. (2002). 'Environment, economy, and society: fitting them together into sustainable development, *Sustainable Development,* Vol. 10, No. 4, pp.187–196.

Kala, M. & Sharma, A. (2010). 'Traditional Indian beliefs: a key toward sustainable living', *The Environmentalist,* Vol. 30, No. 1, pp.85–89.

Devall, W. & Sessions, G. (1985). *Deep Ecology: Living as if Nature Mattered,* Peregrine Smith, Salt Lake City, UT.

Rajvanshi, A. K. (2005). Nature Conservation, Spirituality & Sustainability, Nimbkar Agricultural Research Institute (NARI), P.O. Box 44, Phaltan – 415523, Maharashtra, India, E-mail: anilrajvanshi@gmail.com.

Berry, W. (1979). 'The Gift of Good Land', in W. Berry (Ed), *The Gift of Good Land: Further Essays Cultural and Agricultural,* pp. 67281. San Francisco: North Point Press.

Dhiman, S., & Marques, J. (Eds.). (2016). *Spirituality and Sustainability:* New *Horizons and Exemplary Approaches,* Book.

McDonald, S. (2018). "I too, am Earth: Religion, Spirituality, and Sustainability as Transformative, Themes", Sakenya, Thesis.

Gnanadason, A. (1991). "A Spirituality that sustains us in our struggle", *Voices from the Third World,* Vol. XIV, No.1, p. 78.

Isizoh, C. D. (1998). "Reflecting on Tribal Values", *Indian Journal of Spirituality,* Vol. XI, No. 1, pp. 124f.

Ekka, M. (2011). "The Uniqueness of Indigenous Spirituality-Adivasi Perspective", Unpublished paper presented at the International Theological Symposium on "Indigenous Theology of Asia-Towards New Frontiers", jointly organised by WCC, NCCI, Nagpur, SCEPTRE, Gossner Theological College, Ranchi, and Bishop's College, Kolkata at SCEPTRE, Kolkata, p.11.

Longcaer, A. W. (2010). Quoted in Maria Chavez Quispe, "Affirming Spiritualities of life: Indigenous Peoples' Wisdom and Traditions in Theological Conversation", World Council of Churches: Indigenous Peoples' Programme, Just and Inclusive Communities Geneva: WCC, 2010.

Shrivastava, A. & Kothari, A. (2012). *Churning the Earth: The Making of Global India,* New Delhi: Penguin.

Lakra, J. (2005). *Tribal Spirituality: A Way of Life. Ranchi:* Catholic Press, pp. 2-9; "Adivasi Spirituality", Third Millenium, VIII, 4, pp. 24-39.

Kullu, P. (1996). "Tribal Spirituality: An Integrated Life with Belief", Sevartham, 1996, p. 109.

Tirkey, B. (1980). *Oraon Symbols,* Delhi: *Vidyajyoti,* 1980, pp. 29-31.

Matlock, D. & Jurin, R. (2016). Spirituality and Sustainability Education: A Natural Partnership, Published Online: 21 Dec, https://doi.org/10.1089/sus.2016.29070.dm.

# 7

# Folk narratives and broken environmental clocks of the Nagas

**Mhasileno Peseyie & Rashmi Gaur**

## Introduction

Nagaland is one of the eight North-Eastern states in India with 16 recognised indigenous tribes with a unique and rich terrestrial diversity of flora and fauna supporting diverse agricultural practices and tribal groups. The Nagas depend on a wide variety of plants, animals, species of herbs, fruits and vegetables, and other natural resources, which has helped maintain the Nagas concept of the natural environment (Changkija, 1996; Nienu, 2015). Moreover, respect for nature is deeply embedded in their rich folklore and folk songs linking with their cultural development, survival, beliefs, spirituality, and medicinal systems (Head et al., 2005). Similarly, to other indigenous societies, the Naga's indigenous knowledge was the way of life for all the aspects of the community.

For decades, indigenous knowledge has bound together and continued interacting with the Nagas and nature (Nienu, 2015; Martemjen, 2017). While some dissimilarities between Naga tribal practices (Nienu, 2015; Aier, 2018; Kire, 2019), their cultures and beliefs have become significantly intertwined in their folk narratives (Ao, 1999; Nienu, 2015; Kire, 2019). The folk narratives are especially true in their relationship to the tribe's customary practices (Aier, 2018) formed by indigenous beliefs. Such folk narratives passed on are prescriptive and instructive, containing the statement "that is why we always do this in this manner" (Aier, 2018, p. 3), justifying and reaffirming the continuity of indigenous ways (Aier, 2018).

In a modern and increasingly globalised era, changes in the environment are rapid. For the Nagas, the seasonal cycle and nature have become broken due to climate change. The Nagas indigenous knowledge can express the collective consciousness in understanding the broken rhythm symbolically and culturally. Engaging folktales express the collective consciousness of the local knowledge concerning their beliefs, customs, and traditions. Therefore, this paper aims to provide insight into the folk narratives in protecting the community's sacred environment and the applicability of integrated indigenous traditional knowledge.

## Folk narratives: Naga folktales

Folklorist Elliott Oring (1986) explains the notion of folk narratives as based upon conceptualised narratives that are oral. Such folk narratives exhibit specific characteristics such as "exist[ing] in multiple versions", being re-created with each telling, manifested both the "past language, symbols, events, and forms as well as the present" for a meaningful narration (Oring, 1986, p. 123). Moreover, "folk narrative reflects both the individual and the community" (Oring, 1986, p. 123). Folklorist William Bascom further recognises several categories of folk narratives such as a myth, legend, and folktale (Bascom, 1965). Identically, the Nagas' folk narratives formed the meanings in the people's ethnography and their cultural ethos (Aier, 2018) found in their myths, legends, and folktales.

One such genre of folk narratives is a folktale. A folktale is a related narrative received as a fiction or fantasy (Oring, 1986). It contains wisdom, experiences, and the values of a culture (Samovar et al., 2007). According to writer Temsula Ao (1999), the Naga folktales are those narratives that are "chronological observations of man about life in general and about the life of nature around him" (Ao, 1999, p. 105). Folktales have helped the Naga people understand and communicate coherently among the villagers and clan members. They are "community-owned" (E. Kire, personal communication, April 27, 2020) and reflect cultural beliefs, identity, traditions, and social customs. Besides, the Naga folktales act as a tool for transferring, disseminating, and improving understanding of indigenous knowledge.

## Indigenous knowledge

Indigenous knowledge refers to the cultural skills, beliefs and customs established by local communities in interaction and experiences with their natural surroundings, according to the UNESCO's programme on Local and Indigenous Knowledge Systems (LINKS). According to Imsong (2011), the Nagas, through their indigenous knowledge and culture, give conscious effort to conserve tradition while cultivating transformation, and such knowledge has endured over centuries. The Nagas' historical and cultural context with indigenous knowledge and wisdom ensured a mechanism for ecological balance and sustainability (Konyak, 2018), with a strong sense of physical and spiritual attachment with nature (Imsong, 2011; Longkumer, 2014; Bain, 2017). Indigenous knowledge also has governance value (Whyte, 2018), such as the supernatural forces held "sacred" believed to control the mountains, hills, and rivers (Nienu, 2015). For the Nagas, nature becomes part of their life and livelihood, manifested through their cultural traditions, beliefs, practices, and worldviews expressed through folktales (Bain, 2017).

Therefore, indigenous knowledge practices in their folktales also reflect their plants, herbs, forests, and animals (Konyak, 2018; Zhimomi, 2020) as cultural knowledge about their environment. Consequently, the Nagas can be a prime example of continuous interaction with people and nature with all its endowments (Longkumer, 2014). However, many Naga communities have gradually modernised and rejected such indigenous knowledge, viewing it as backward and primitive (Thong, 2012). Despite such changes, indigenous knowledge has helped them imagine and situate a universalising impulse towards preserving their environment.

## What is an Environmental clock?

Following a continuous mode of natural seasonal cycles among the Nagas for sustainable living is common. This illusionary seasonal clock used by the Nagas can be referred to as the "environmental clock". The term "environmental clock" was developed by Literature Professor Paul Huebener (2020) in *Nature's Broken Clocks*. He understands that in the era of climate change and environmental collapse, the stories we tell ourselves, following timings of the natural world, are essential. The figurative clock that ticks all around us, forming time within ecosystems and human cultures, contains great potential for imaginative responses and reconstruction (Huebener, 2020).

Situating the clock within the Nagas comforts the indigenous community with clarity and purpose in a bewildering world that deserves to be valued (Huebener, 2020). The Nagas firmly uphold the traditional parallel practices of sowing seeds, harvesting, hunting, fishing, gathering herbs denoted through sayings and indications of the seasonal cycle. Therefore, these shared elements between men, nature and religious beliefs created favourable environmental relations for centuries. The Nagas' environment, agricultural activities, and social lives are intertwined in a cycle usually made known through their folktales. Folktales have helped the Nagas understand and follow the cycle.

As the literature scholar Mark Currie (2007) observes, every story knows something about time. The Nagas' folktale reveals "time" in its truest sense with forecast images of time, changes, indications in the seasonal cycle of Nagaland. Today, the use of indigenous knowledge as a common factor to establish their adaptive behaviours, especially the Nagas' seasonal timings, can also play an essential role in the larger realm of their existence within their communities. Hence, this paper will give an insight into the folk narratives in protecting the community's sacred environment and the applicability of integrated indigenous traditional knowledge.

## Theoretical Framework and Research Method

In this study, the folktales selected are evident from the abundance and variants of the tribal lore. Therefore, select Naga Folktales are analyzed through the theoretical framework of folk narratives and interpretative content analysis. Many folk narratives aim to establish themselves in multiple versions including the past language, symbols, events, and forms, as well as the present for a meaningful narration. Folk narratives also reflect both the individual and the community (Oring, 1986). The content analysis aims to elicit the indigenous knowledge directly, cultural beliefs, customs, and traditions through the Naga folktales (Nienu, 2015; Aier, 2018). Through this analysis, it is possible to gather folktales as data under indigenous knowledge themes. All the folktales selected here were analyzed to better understand the harmonisation of indigenous knowledge and experiences across the Naga community and how to cope with environmental changes.

For this study, ten Naga folktales were chosen (see Table 1) based on a theme or subtheme of the relationship between environment and indigenous knowledge of the Nagas. The tales were taken from the first collections of *Folktales from Nagaland* by P.K Bhattacharya (1971), and *Fables from the Misty Mountains: Folklore of The Nagas* compiled by the Department of Art and Culture, Government of Nagaland (2009). All folktales in the collection are retold and translated from different tribes in English. These folktales were disseminated through the Nagas institution, such as the *morung*. The Government of Nagaland published these folktales chosen here to preserve the Nagas' folk culture, and literature can indicate that they are authentic.

## Naga indigenous knowledge in the folktales

The select Naga folktales variations from different Naga tribes are analyzed to narrate the use of indigenous knowledge by the Nagas. The folktales employ the indigenous knowledge as a guide and establish the moral messages, including conserving their environment, which is delivered through the characters and practices, either explicitly or implicitly. The theme formed good characteristics in the Naga community, firmly embedded in the tales (as shown in Table 1).

**Table 1. Lists of the Naga folktales using indigenous knowledge-related themes.**

| Title of the folktale | Tribe | Theme of the Indigenous Knowledge |
|---|---|---|
| *Kaso Apfu* | Sema | Time of sowing seeds |
| Three brothers | Angami | Relationship between man, nature, and spirit |
| The story of *Pfukha* and *Sikha* | Zeliang | Natural millet cultivation |
| *Longkongla* | Ao | Traditional poisoning of fishing |
| The lady vanishes | Sangtam | Never to misuse the river and all the life forms |
| When lizards cry | Phom | Lizards cry *Monyek!* correspond with July, the hottest month |
| The orphan and the elephant | Chang | Herbs used as medicine |
| Eyeball of Heaven | Konyak | Community fishing using *Kaai yak* |
| Two friends who went to catch hornbill | — | Use of small bamboo sticks to climb a tree trunk |
| The Advice of an old man | Angami | Indigenous wisdom saving the village |

In the context of the environmental clock of the Nagas, the Sema variant of folktale *Kaso-Apfu* focuses on *Kaso*, a youngster who heeds the words of his dying father to ensure food security by sowing seeds following natural cyclical seasons. *Kaso* asked his father,

> How am I to know the time and season of sowing seeds in the field? Tell me the time of the season of sowing seeds? *Kaso's* dying father then told him, 'I will come in the form of a bird every year to tell you the right time of sowing season'. *Kaso-Apfu! Kaso-Apfu*! As such, when you hear this voice, you should sow your seeds in your field! Having said this, *Kaso-Apfu* breathed his last. The *Kaso-Apfu* bird, known as a cuckoo in English, thus became a seasoned bird, which comes singing every year in time (Bhattacharya, 1971, p. 68).

*Kaso* was convinced that his father had turned into a bird and advised him when it was "time" for sowing seeds. He obeyed his father and filled his basket with seeds and went to the field. *Kaso* was able to obtain a good harvest. Hence, whenever the cuckoo crowed, villagers knew that it was time to sow seeds. This relationship focuses on the connection between indigenous sayings and stories told by elders using a bird as an environmental clock that carries the community's identity.

The Angami tribe variations of the tale *Three brothers*- man, tiger, and the spirit are some of the most popular tales. The narrative reflects the trio relationship between- humans, animals, and the supernatural. Bhattacharya (1971) reveals,

> In times past, man, tiger, and spirit were brothers who all lived peacefully together. Amongst them, the tiger was the eldest, next the spirit and man the youngest. (Bhattacharya, 1971, p. 7)

However, as days passed by after their parents both died, they decided to separate their ways. The spirit plans with his younger brother, the man, and devises a plan to chase away the tiger to the jungle. Various elements can be understood from the tale's narratives, such as the mythical family and the concept of brotherhood. The Naga's ancestral connection with such narratives has both horizontal and vertical dimensions (Nienu, 2015), especially it has created harmony and respect among the different creations on earth.

The Zeliang tale of *Pfukha and Sikha* focuses on a young orphan boy whom his uncle advised to cultivate millet to pay all his debts.

> The boy cleared up a large tract of land and cultivated millet. The harvest was unexpectedly abundant that he could not bring home all alone. (Bhattacharya, 1971, p. 10)

The young boy worked hard and naturally, grew millet while not disturbing the ecological balance. In this kind of cultivation, "the trees are felled, and the twigs and leaves are burnt so that the ash provides good manure" (Kire, 2019, p. 38). It brought him an abundant harvest. However, his niece was envious of his granaries filled with millets and burnt down all his grains. Therefore, the young boy ran away to another village adopted by *Pfukha* and lived a prosperous, happy life. Here we can understand that when the Nagas maintained balance and harmony with nature, a "state of ideal equilibrium" (Nienu, 2015, p. 34), the fertility of crops increased, believed to be controlled by the supernatural forces (Nienu, 2015). The millets are one of the important staple foods for the Nagas.

The folktale of *Longkongla* from the Ao tribe similarly talks about the Naga traditional fishing, which helps in conservation; however, the tale has a tragic ending. *Longkongla's* grandson *Tsungpi,* who grew up to be exceedingly handsome, winning the hearts of many girls in the village, created envy and jealousy among the men folks who conspired to kill him.

As pre-planned, one day, they went down to a river on the pretext of poisoning fish. On request, *Tsungpi* and his best friend *Tsitiyong* accompanied them. On reaching the river, they asked *Tsitiyong* to go down to the other end of the stream and remain there watching dying fishes floating down due to poisoning upstream. Soon after he left, they began pounding fish poison in the baskets they carried and asked *Tsungpi* to pour water in those baskets. (Bhattacharya, 1971, p. 2). Eventually, *Tsungpi*, without knowing their intention, was busy pouring water in the basket while the other boys forcibly pushed him into a basket and pounded him. *Longkongla*, hearing the treacherous act, took revenge on the villagers while the spirit helped her. However, *Longkongla* died because she could not follow the end instructions given by the spirit. This tale contains indigenous ways of traditional fishing, and such fishing time by menfolk rebuilt relationships with the river ecosystem, invoke blessings from God upon the aquatic lives and abstain from misusing the river for the rest of the year (Martemjen, 2017). A similar tale on the theme is, *the lady vanishes*, where it explores the supernatural elements and relationship of the Nagas towards its environment. The tale explores *Thra's* village, when the god of the river was angry and turned turbulent, threatening to submerge their village because some unruly boys ignored the warning and violated the sanctity of the river. The whole village was scared and tried to pacify the angry river god, but it was vain. Just then, *Thra's* mother said:

> "I'm confident of pacifying the river, but you must first promise not to misuse the river and all the life forms it sustains," …so saying, she dived into the river, never to be seen again. The body of water receded, and the villagers were saved from drowning to death. Many believed *Thra's* mother turned into a fish to guard the river against pollution. (GON, 2009, p. 148).

Therefore, the moral of the story is that "defiling nature is like tainting your mother" (GON, 2009, p. 148). Such behaviour disturbs the Naga environmental clock because reverence for nature and all its life forms is the basis of the local tribes. The Nagas feared nature's existence has mystic power, and it can be life-threatening when disobeyed or disturbed.

Among the Phom, a Naga tribe, it is believed that *Lizards cry* in July. This narrative was considered among the tribe because such beliefs can dictate their agricultural activities (Martemjen, 2018). This tale is narrated since, in this month, a poor little girl was forced to become a lizard. Once upon a time, the little girl's grandmother realised that there were food deprivations, and the little girl was the reason she did not have enough to eat. There was an extreme food shortage in the family at that time. On a bad day, wicked grandma threw boiling hot water on the little girl, and the girl screamed *"Monyek, Monyek*" as her body shrunk and turned into a lizard. Hence, *Monyek* corresponds with July, arguably the hottest month in the Naga domain (GON, 2009).

The tragic tale of the *Orphan and the Elephant* is narrated among the Chang tribe. There was an orphan boy in the village whom an elephant swallowed. Fortunately, he carried with him a *dao* (a Naga knife) and slowly was able to kill the elephant from the inside after surviving three days inside the stomach. However, after he came out, his body was filled with flies and ailments, for which he got a "medicinal leaf" from a tree called *mempo* and removed all the flies and felt better. Consequently, his *dao* was used by the spirits who threw back at the boy and killed him. Probably the boy could not follow as Kire (2019) observed, the importance of the Naga ritual of "spirit appeasement or propitiation after killing any wild animals" (Kire, 2019, p. 46). These are the tales where the Nagas are warned against being careful. It is part of their environmental clock where the Naga mind accepts the natural and the spiritual world (Kire, 2019). Similarly, another theme also indicates that the Nagas used natural herbs to cure ailments as part of indigenous knowledge.

Community fishing among the Konyak tribe has been practiced for generations. The tale variation of *Eyeball of Heaven* explores tribal fishing using *Kaai yak* leaf as important indigenous knowledge practices whenever the time is open for fishing.

> Community fishing entails beating the surface of a river with a certain kind of leaf (Kaai yak). These leaves release toxins that stun the fish but are not harmful to humans. (GON, 2009, p. 152)

This tale shows a narrative about a widow's son who went community fishing with adult villagers but was killed by animals when gone to fetch the leaves for fishing. Unfortunately, only his eyeballs remain, which his mother threw up to heaven and believed to have turned into a star. According to the Nagas, community fishing is not just a practice but plays a vital role in their social and cultural life (Martemjen, 2017). However, it does not occur regularly and is declining due to environmental changes (Martemjen, 2017).

A similar theme of indigenous ways of trapping or catching birds, which were common activities among the Nagas, is also visible in the tale *Two friends who went to catch hornbill*. The friends used "small bamboo sticks and fixed one after another on the tree trunk to climb the tree" (Bhattacharya, 1971, p. 75) to get the hornbill chicks in the nest. Interestingly, the hornbill is known as the "queen of the birds" (Nienu, 2015, p. 258) by the Konyak tribe, and the Nagas use its tail feather as a symbol of a victorious warrior. Here it is demonstrated that the Nagas indigenous ways of trapping birds without disturbing the nest or cutting the trees in the forests indicated their responsibility for conserving trees or birds. Moreover, The Nagas are forbidden to cut certain sacred trees, such as oak, banyan, peepul, etc. (Martemjen, 2017).

The Nagas' indigenous knowledge offers a precise way of surviving and adapting within the indigenous world. The Nagas are carriers of ancestral knowledge and wisdom about their biodiversity. They are responsible for preserving and maintaining traditional knowledge and the environmental cycle (Martemjen, 2017). One such popular tale among the Angami tribe is the *Advice of an old man*. The following excerpt explains how the old man's advice saved the village in times of inter-village disputes.

> Many years ago, it is said, a fire broke out somewhere near a village by the name Dihoma. The fire spread out as far as the Mao territory and gutted many houses in a village there. The Mao people held the residents of Dihoma collectively responsible for the incident being unable to detect the culprit. They filed a case against the people of Dihoma accordingly. A day was then fixed for the trial.
>
> ...there was an old man in Dihoma who could not attend the trial himself owing to his advanced age therefore asked a young boy of the village and advised the boy on how to defend the case.
>
> ... "none can deny that the fire broke out somewhere from our village area. So, we ought to pay off the compensation as per traditional bindings. But with one condition- The Mao people should also compensate for the loss caused to our village every year as a result of the flood occurring from the river which arises from their area". (Bhattacharya, 1971, p. 27)

The case was settled mutually as the Mao people had no reason to refute at the point put forward. Hence, Dihoma village was saved. The given case demonstrates the wise old man using indigenous experience, which evolves through time and involves constant learning-by-doing and experimenting (Berkes, 2008). Though varied traditional ways may not be followed today for sustenance, the Nagas are still the custodians of knowledge about them.

These folktales reflect the ethos of the Nagas society. Ben- Amos (1969) reveals that "folktales have thematic entities" (Ben-Amos, 1969, p. 279), forming complete meaning on their own. Nevertheless, the Nagas comprise many tribes, and each tribe abounds with their distinctive and tribe-specific folktales. Among which "traditions and memories of that particular village (tribe) was preserved and narrated with clarity" (Aier, 2018, p. 11). Culture and indigenous knowledge are universal through the Nagas folktales, and many storytellers' efforts to imagine and narrate resilience towards local practices attached to their environment are recognised.

After engaging these Naga folktales, it is established that the Nagas are spiritual beings. They believe that forests are the abode of spirits, animals, and rivers. Since there are indwelling spirits in their environment, the Nagas thanked the forests for all the products and provisions they received from them. Furthermore, such symbolical beliefs among the Naga cultures directly link with the positive energy and reverence for nature and their environment. The Nagas' environmental clock denotes how the Naga believe their seasonal timings fall during different times of the year. The Nagas' perception that God converses to them through nature is an interim indicator of time, season, and weather (Martemjen, 2017). It also allows the Nagas to closely follow such beliefs about the natural timings because there was no mechanical clock. Besides, the Nagas relation with the natural world is sustained through balance in the environmental clock.

Likewise, it is observed that such an environment and culture clock of the Nagas have become broken, and "everyday narratives" such as the folktales must reveal the "way we talk about natural time" (Huebener, 2020, p. 3). As a result, folktales allow the preservation of indigenous knowledge, which potentially can help the Nagas from different disciplines and domains better understand the Nagas indigenous world and how one can work on "applied environmental problems" (M. Moezzi et al., 2017, p. 2). Indigenous peoples' relationships to the environment examine the importance of indigenous knowledge and provide models for a time-tested form of sustainability needed in the world today (Nelson & Shilling, 2018). The Nagas should go back to the cultural practices of indigenous traditional knowledge in the civilising and mystical sense of the word, revered by the communities, and frame a new ecological understanding.

## Conclusion

This paper discusses the Naga folktales embedded with environment-related themes in promoting indigenous knowledge, which can play a vital role in adaptation effort and climate change assessment. The Nagas' culture is strengthened by its folktales, manifested in their sacredness towards preserving the ecosystem. These recurrent themes indicated in the Naga folktales can help conserve the community's environment through the ethos of folktales and give a better understanding of the application of integrated indigenous knowledge towards climate change.

## References


Aier, A. (2018). *Studies on naga oral tradition: Memories and telling of origin myth and migration*. Heritage publishing house.

Ao, T. (1999). *The ao-naga oral tradition*. Bhasha Publications.

Bain, W. K. (2017). Conservation of environment through traditional knowledge and wisdom with special reference to beliefs and practices in tribal India: An overview. *Journal of Multidisciplinary Studies in Archaeology*, 5, 224-243. https://www.researchgate.net/publication/340426988

Bascom, W. (1965). The forms of folklore: Prose narratives. *The Journal of American Folklore*, 78(307), 3-20. https://www.jstor.org/stable/538099

Ben-Amos, D. (1969). Analytical categories and ethnic genres. *Genre*, 2 (3), 275-301. https://repository.upenn.edu/nelc_papers/143

Berkes, F. (2008). *Sacred ecology: traditional ecological knowledge and resource management*. Routledge.

Bhattacharya, P.K. (1971). *Folktales from Nagaland*. Naga Institute of Culture.

Changkija, S. (1996). Biodiversity of the northeast India. *Proceedings of wildlife festival of Nagaland.* Kohima.

Currie, M. (2007). *About time: Narrative, fiction, and the philosophy of time*. Edinburgh University Press.

Department of art and culture. (2009). *Fables from the misty mountains: Folklore of the nagas*. Government of Nagaland & LBS Publications.

Head, L., Trigger, D., and Mulcock, J. (2005). Culture as concept and influence in environmental research and management. *Conservation and Society*, 3(2), 251–264. https://www.jstor.org/stable/pdf/26396578.pdf

Imsong, M. (2011). *God, land, people: An ethnic naga identity*. Heritage Publishing House.

Huebener, P. (2020). *Nature's broken clocks: Reimaging time in the face of the environmental crisis*. University Regina Press.

Kire, E. (2019). *Walking the roadless road: Exploring the tribes of Nagaland*. Rupa Publications India.

Konyak, E. (2018, January 9). Respecting nature and social responsibility. *Eastern Mirror*. https://easternmirrornagaland.com/respecting-nature-and-social-responsibility/

Longkumer, L., and Martemjen. (2014). Biodiversity conservation ethos in naga folklore and folk songs. *International Journal of Advanced Research*, 2(5), 1008-1013. https://www.journalijar.com/uploads/758_IJAR-3397.pdf

Martemjen. (2017). *Biodiversity conservation, indigenous knowledge, and practices: A naga perspective*. Notion Press.

Moezzi, M., Janda, K.B., Rotmann, S. (2017). Using stories, narratives, and storytelling in energy and climate change research. *Energy Research & Social Science*. 31, 1-10. https://doi.org/10.1016/j.erss.2017.06.034

Nelson, M. K., & Shilling, D. (Ed.). (2018). *Traditional ecological knowledge: Learning from indigenous practices for environmental sustainability*. Cambridge University Press.

Nienu, V. (2015). *Naga cultural milieu, An adaptation to mountain ecosystem*. Thomson Press.

Oring, E. (1986). *Folk groups and folklore genres: An introduction*. Utah State University Press.

Samovar, L.A., Porter, R.E., McDaniel, E.R. (2009). *Communication between cultures* (7th Ed.). Wadsworth, Cengage Learning.

Thong, T. (2012). To raise the savage to a higher level: The westernisation of nagas and their culture. *Modern Asian Studies*, 46(4), 893–918. https://doi:10.1017/S0026749X11000412

UNESCO. (n.d.). *Local and indigenous knowledge systems*. https://en.unesco.org/links

Whyte, K. (2018). What do indigenous knowledges do for indigenous peoples? In M.K. Nelson and D. Shilling (Ed.), *Traditional ecological knowledge: Learning from indigenous practices for environmental sustainability* (pp. 57-82). Cambridge University Press.

Zhimomi, I. (2020, March 6). Revive traditional conservation practices. *Nagaland post*. https://www.nagalandpost.com/revive-traditional-conservation-practices/216558.html

# 8

# Indigenous Knowledge in Natural Resource Management: An Observation of the Practices among Nyishi Tribe of Arunachal Pradesh

**Tame Ramya**


### Abstract

Arunachal Pradesh, which covers a considerable portion of India's forest areas, is rich in biological diversity regarding flora, fauna, and ethnicity. Several tribal communities contribute to the state's cultural heritage. This exploratory study was carried out in Nyapin CD Block in Kurung Kumey district to document Indigenous Knowledge (IK) used by the Nyishi tribe in their daily activities, focusing on the traditional use of forests and other natural resources. The study area was chosen because it is one of the most remote forested areas where people continue to rely on natural resources. Seventy-five households were evaluated using various participatory appraisals administered via a semi-structured questionnaire. The respondents were farmers who lived on hilltops and hill slopes in a pristine environment, surrounded by high ranges of hills and dense forests. They developed their IK by practicing *jhum* (shifting cultivation) and other land use systems and utilising natural resources. In most cases, such IK has become an essential factor in the sustainable management of their forest resources. With this, there is a need to investigate the lifestyle and ethno-forestry perceptions governed by IK governing the daily activities of ethnic communities to conserve them and assess the possibilities for conserving forest resources by utilising such traditional indigenous concepts.

***Keywords:*** Nyishi Tribe, Kurung Kumey, Ethno-Forestry, Forest Resources, *Jhum*, Sustainability.

## Introduction

The tribal population of the world is estimated at more than 370 million people found in more than 70 countries (ILO, 2019). In India, 705 ethnic groups are recognised as Scheduled Tribes, usually referred to as *Adivasis* in Central India, which means Indigenous Peoples.[13] With an estimated population of 104 million, they comprise 8.6 percent of the country's total population (*IWGIA,* 2020). There are, however, many more ethnic groups that would qualify for Scheduled Tribe status but which are not officially recognised. As a result, estimates of the total number of tribal groups are higher than the official figure. The largest concentrations of Indigenous Peoples are found in the seven states of Northeast India, and the so-called "central tribal belt" stretches from Rajasthan to West Bengal.

From time immemorial tribal people have lived beside the forest that, with its multitudinous uses, is intimately connected with their life (Samal, 1997; Dwivedi, 1993). Such services from the forest have played a vital role in the economy of the tribes in Arunachal Pradesh. Their religious, cultural, and economic activities depend on their forests. In other words, traditional mountain societies are characterised by their close interconnection with nature and natural resources (Ramakrishnan, 2007). They generally depend upon natural resources and biodiversity for their sustainable livelihood (Ramakrishnan, 1992; Ramakrishnan et al., 1994; Ramakrishnan et al., 1996). This relationship extends beyond the biophysical ecology and economic concerns; social, cultural, and spiritual dimensions also play a significant role (Ramakrishnan et al., 1998).

The Kurung Kumey district, the study site, is inhabited by three tribal communities viz. Nyishi, Bangru, and Puroik (Ramya, 2014a; 2014b). For centuries, these tribal communities have been living on slash-and-burn agriculture or *Jhum* cultivation (locally called *Tumph-Rungo*), fishing, hunting, and harvesting forest products. The Nyishi is one of the major ethnic communities of Arunachal Pradesh who exhibit a different socio-political and cultural organisation compared to other tribal groups (Fig. 1). They live in hamlets (Fig. 2), small settlements comprising five to fifty households usually sited on the hill slopes, which are the primary socio-economic units of Nyishi life. The houses are built on high wooden or bamboo platforms. The house is built wholly of natural materials like bamboo, wood, cane, wild grasses, wild banana leaves, etc., that are readily available from the forest. In exploiting forest products, the Nyishi apply their knowledge traditionally transmitted from their precursors.

Ideal knowledge is generally derived from abstract principles by systematic deduction (Pramukh & Palkumar, 2006). However, indigenous knowledge (IK) refers to knowledge that is generated and transmitted by communities over time to cope with their own agroecological and

**Fig. 1: A Typical Nyishi Woman and Child in Front of a Dwelling House.**

socio-economic environments. It is transmitted through stories, folk songs, folk literature, and practice owing to enculturation (Masreque & Khan, 2000). It develops through experience sharing and passes typically on through generations by oral expressions and persists in an unwritten form.

According to Atran (1999), IK structures are like scientific theories in that they generalise from concrete experience, but unlike theories, they are not systematic formulations. Instead, they involve adjusting forms of human livelihood to the environment in which they are embedded. Oviedo and Mafi (2000) stated that the knowledge, innovations, and practices of indigenous peoples and traditional communities are part and parcel of their cultures. It is essential not just in terms of the description, proper management, and harvesting of a product; but also in the maintenance of ecological processes and biodiversity linked to traditional economic activities such as cultivation or animal husbandry (Larsen, 2000). The ethnic communities not only know about various uses of plant diversity but are also aware of biological aspects of plants, e.g., growth, lowering times, seed formation, propagation method, valuable parts, and varietals/genotypic differences in indigenous uses.

Most indigenous communities care about their surrounding environment and apply various systems and practices to deal with land resources, wildlife, plants, and water (Larsen, 2000). When people are compelled to live in challenging situations like rugged forest areas, they have no option but to depend on natural resources for their livelihoods. In these situations, the traditional communities evolve strategies to effectively harmonize their resources (Singh, 2004). Almost all the ethnic communities in the Kurung Kumey district have developed indigenous knowledge systems, practicing special patterns of the utilisation of forest products.

**Fig. 2: A Typical Nyishi Hamlet inside Deep Hill Forest.**

Although several studies have been carried out on various aspects of other tribes of the Kurung Kumey district, no previous study on indigenous knowledge systems has been done due to the isolation and inaccessibility of the Nyishi community. Therefore, this study was undertaken to ascertain and document the natural resource management system of the Nyishi tribe and their impact on the sustainability of the natural resources in the Kurung Kumey district of Arunachal Pradesh.

## Materials and Methods

*Study Site*

The study was conducted in three Nyishi villages, i.e., Hiya, Lumtey, and Yarda located in the Nyapin circle of Kurung Kumey district of

Arunachal Pradesh (Fig. 3). Nyapin circle, locally known as *Nyoping*, occupies an area of 275 sq. km mostly forest barring a few valleys and river basins. With an altitude of 2,426 metres (7,959 ft.) above sea level, it lies at 27°8' North Latitude and 93°33' East Longitude. Nyapin, about 56 km south of Koloriang, the district headquarters of Kurung Kumey is one of the remotest circles of Arunachal Pradesh. As of 2011, the circle has a total population of 6,651, mainly consisting of the Nyishi tribe. As far as sample villages are concerned, Hiya village has 64 households with a population of 402, with 193 males and 209 females. Lumtey, consisting of 43 households, has a population of 283, of which 141 are males while 142 are females; Yarda village, with 70 households, has a population of 433, of which 207 are males while 226 are females.

## *Methods*

Through the purposive sampling method, three Nyishi hamlets were selected from the Nyishi villages in the Nyapin circle. From each of the three hamlets, 25 households were selected randomly. Thus, a total of 75 households were selected from the study area.

A preliminary discussion was carried out with members of the village panchayat, the Head Gaon Burah (HGB) of the respective hamlets, and the members of the farmers before the household sampling began. Interview techniques were employed to elicit information and IK on managing shifting cultivation; daily life activities; collection, processing and management of forest produce and other resources. An open-ended semi-structured questionnaire was used for the survey. Since this research was mainly qualitative, emphasis was given to information concerning the utilisation of natural resources in the community's way. The main questions consist of; what resources they collect from the forest, how they process the raw products, how they manage their main crop production system (shifting cultivation) and so on. Side by side, physical observations of practices embodying some IK were also made. Household heads were the main respondents in the interviews, helped by other members of the family when necessary. The information gathered was arranged systematically and documented as 'qualitative descriptions'.

**Hiya Village**

**Yarda Village**

**Lumtey Village**

***Source:*** https://www.google.com/earth/

**Fig. 3: Maps Showing the Sample Villages.**

## Results

### *Indigenous Knowledge (IK) Practices*

The survey shows that the Nyishi employed several indigenous knowledge (IK) practices inherited from their forefathers in everyday activities in every aspect of their life and promoted them, either with intent or inadvertently, within their society. The indigenous knowledge (IK) practice by the people can be summarised as under:

### *Consumption of Edible Plants from Forests*

Despite their agriculture, the tradition of eating wild plants has remained in the indigenous communities. These plants, whose various parts were eaten by the Nyishi people, were reported to be collected exclusively from the surrounding forests. In some cases, only one of the parts was used; in others, more than one part was edible, and the whole plant was used in their daily diet. The mode of use was viewed as one of the important aspects of their IK. The Nyishi were found to use the following plants for various purposes.

The root of yam (*Dioscorea sp.*), locally known as *Inyi*, and Taro (*Colocasia esculenta*), known as *Aal*, were used as vegetables. Young shoots (locally termed as *Iigh*) of different bamboo species were cooked as vegetables. These shoots were, to some extent, bitter. They are consumed mainly between July to September. The part eaten was the tender part of the rhizome apex and very immature culm – consisting of compressed internodes protected by many leathery sheaths. After removing the sheaths, the inner tender portion was thoroughly washed in water, cut into pieces, and cooked as a vegetable. These parts were also observed to be sliced and dried to preserve for use in times of food scarcity.

There are several varieties of *Kupak* (domesticated bananas) and *Kulung* or *Kuduk* (wild bananas) in the *Jhum* lands and forest areas of the hill tracts. After peeling off the outer skin of the stem from the plants of ripe bananas, the *Pakring* (the white spongy core) was used as a vegetable by the Nyishi. The hair-like strings from the softcore were removed to make them easier to eat. The inflorescence of the wild banana is also reported to be cooked and eaten as vegetables. The farmers opined that they frequently used these wild banana fruits for medicinal purposes, particularly for treating dysentery and diarrhoea. Apart from the plant described above, numerous species are used as vegetables and medicines to cure various ailments. The plant species are given in Table 1.

### *Plants Used as Ethnomedicines*

The Nyishi tribe of Arunachal Pradesh have a rich legacy of using indigenous plants to treat various ailments (Tripathi et al., 2017). As such, it was evident from the survey that the Nyishi were significantly dependent on herbal medicine. Because of their aloofness towards modern medical practices due to their pristine living style and the absence of facilities and services because of inaccessibility, they depend on indigenous ethnomedicines, generally prepared from the plants available in the adjacent forests. Besides, medicinal plants grown in traditional agroforestry systems bear ecological and social values (Deb et al., 2009). They have a great understanding of plants possessing medicinal properties too. Almost every elder in the hamlets was found to be knowledgeable about the medicinal value of some plants. Usually, those species treat common diseases like coughs, colds, fevers, headaches, stomach pains, toothache, joint aches, diarrhoea, dysentery, minor wounds and cuts, etc. A total of 25 plant species, including herbs, shrubs, climbers, plants, and trees (Table 1) were reported to be used frequently by the Nyishi tribe for these purposes.

**Table 1: Medicinal Plants Used by the Nyishi Tribe in Kurung Kumey District, Arunachal Pradesh**

| Sl No. | Species | Family | Common Name | Local Name | Part Used | Uses in Different Ailments |
|---|---|---|---|---|---|---|
| 1. | *Acmella oleracea* | Asteraceae | Toothache Plant/Szechuan Buttons/ Paracress | *Mobu Uw* | The whole plant (stem, leaf, flower) | Used to relieve pain often associated with mouth ulcers, toothache, sore throat, and stomach ache. |
| 2. | *Ageratum conyzoides* | Asteraceae | Billy Goat Weed | *Pasu-Payu* | Leaf | Fresh leaf paste is used to treat fresh wounds caused by burns and cuts. |
| 3. | *Clerodendrum glandulosum* | Lamiaceae | East Indian glory bower | *Poto* | Leaf | Used for the treatment of various ailments and disorders such as cough, dysentery, headache stomach disorder, colic pain, hypertension, helminthic infections, and diabetes. |
| 4. | *Coptis teeta* | Ranunculaceae | Golden Thread Herb | *Rangke* | Rhizome | Used for health problems like loose motion, stomach pain, diarrhoea, and malaria. |
| 5. | *Crassocephalum crepidioides* | Asteraceae | Okinawa Spinach/ Redflower Ragleaf/ Fireweed | *Hubuk/ Babuk* | Leaf, Stem | Used *to treat indigestion, stomach ache, epilepsy, sleeping sickness, and swollen lips.* |
| 6. | *Diplazium esculentum (Retz.) Sw.* | Athyriaceae | | *Huka-Pada/Aka-Lama* | Leaf, Stem | Used for the prevention or treatment of several diseases such as diabetes, smallpox, asthma, diarrhoea, rheumatism, dysentery, headache, fever, wounds, pain, measles, hypertension, constipation, oligospermia, bone fracture, and glandular swellings. |
| 7. | *Fagopyrum esculentum* | Polygonaceae | Buckwheat/Common Buckwheat | *Hukyung* | Rhizom, Leaf, Stem | It helps in reducing plasma cholesterol levels, anti-inflammatory, neuroprotective, anti-cancer, anti-diabetic effects and enhancing hypertension symptoms. |
| 8. | *Garcinia pedunculata* | Clusiaceae | Bor Thekera (Assamese) | *Mwbya/Tabyang* | Fruit | The fruits of Garcinia have been utilized in infusions for treating wounds, ulcers, and dysentery. |
| 9. | *Houttuynia cordata* | Saururaceae | Fish Mint/Fish Leaf/Rainbow Plant/Chameleon Plant | *Hungya* | Root, Leaf | Used to treat pneumonia, hypertension, constipation, and hyperglycaemia via detoxification, reduction of heat and diuretic action. |
| 10. | *Litsea cubeba* | Lauraceae | | *Tayar/Yarkyang* | Fruit | Traditionally used for curing various gastrointestinal ailments (e.g., diarrhoea, stomachache, indigestion, and gastroenteritis) along with diabetes, oedema, cold, arthritis, asthma, and traumatic injury. |
| 11. | *Molineria capitulata* | *Hypoxidaceae* | Palm Grass | *Doyak* | Tuber | Used to stop bleeding from a fresh wound or cut. |
| 12. | *Pilea pumila* | Urticaceae | Clearweed | *Gunggi* | Stem, Leaf | Used to alleviate itching, cure sinus problems, and treat excessive hunger. |
| 13. | *Piper sarmentosum* | Piperaceae | Wild Pepper | *Ryaar* | Leaf | Used to cure skin diseases, rheumatism, headache, diarrhoea, and toothache. |

*(Contd...)*

| | | | | | | |
|---|---|---|---|---|---|---|
| 14. | *Plantago major L.* | Plantaginaceae | Broadleaf Plantain/White Man's Footprint | *Nyad-Nyar* | Leaf | Used as a wound healing remedy, treatment for diseases related to the skin, respiratory organs, digestive organs, reproduction, circulation, against cancer, pain relief and against infections. |
| 15. | *Pouzolzia hirta* | Urticaceae | Oyik (Adi & Galo Vernacular); Husak-Huyak (Nyishi Vernacular) | *Husak-Huyak* | Stem, Leaf | Used to treat boils and abscesses, abdominal cramps in females and leucorrhoea. They are also used to treat bone dislocations and fractures. |
| 16. | *Rhus chinensis* | Anacardiaceae | Chinese Sumac/Nutgall Tree | *Takmu-Musi* | Seed | Used as a medicine for the treatment of gastrointestinal problems, urinary complaints, and many other health ailments like coughs, diarrhoea, night sweats, dysentery, etc. |
| 17. | *Schefflera heptaphylla* | Araliaceae | Umbrella Plant | *Joku* | Leaf | Used as a traditional medicine for the treatment of inflammation, rheumatism, fever, and traumatic bleeding. |
| 18. | *Solanum indicum* | Solanaceae | African Eggplant | *Byake* | Seed | Used for the treatment of asthma, catarrh, dropsy, chest pain, chronic fever, colic, dry and spasmodic cough, oedema, scorpion stings, difficult urination, and worm infestation. |
| 19. | *Solanum nigrum L.* | Solanaceae | Black Nightshade | *Hurey* | Seed | Used for the treatment of bacterial infections, cough and indigestion. |
| 20. | *Solanum torvum* | Solanaceae | Turkey Berry/Pea Eggplant | *Pata Byake* | Fruit, Leaf | Used for the treatment of fever, wounds, tooth decay, reproductive problems, and arterial hypertension. |
| 21. | *Nicotiana tabacum* | Solanaceae | Tobacco | *Mwk/Kwli* | Leaf | Crushed leaves and juice are applied to fresh wounds and cuts to stop bleeding. The young leaf is also applied and tied to the boil to avoid infection as well as to facilitate its early rupturing. |
| 22. | *Zanthoxylum armatum DC.* | Rutaceae | Winged Prickly Ash or Rattan Pepper | *Sana* | Fruit, Stem, Leaf, Bark | Used to cure gas trouble, fever, and appetizer. It is effective to relieve stomach pain, toothache and inflammation. |
| 23. | *Zanthoxylum rhetsa/Zanthoxylum ailanthoides* | Rutaceae | Indian prickly ash | *Hunyar* | Seed, Leaf, Bark | Used for the treatment of dental caries, dizziness and bloating, malaria, urinary diseases, rheumatism, diuretic, stomach ache and diarrhoea. |
| 24. | *Zanthoxylum simulans* | Rutaceae | Szechuan Pepper/Chinese-Pepper | *Hunam* | Seed | It is used in the treatment of gastralgia and dyspepsia due to colds with vomiting, diarrhoea, abdominal pain, ascariasis and dermal diseases. |

**Source:** *Field Survey.*

## Housing and Construction: Plants as the Key Elements

The survey revealed that houses of the Nyishi tribe, locally called *Naam* (Fig. 4), were generally situated on the upper, exposed slopes of the hill. Their houses were much larger than the *Bangru* and *Puroik*, the other two major tribal groups in the Kurung Kumey district. All the houses in the study area were made of wood, bamboo, rattan, wild banana leaves, and sun grass (*Imperata cylindrica*) collected from forests. A wooden staircase (a tree trunk with notched steps), locally called *Abah*, is used in front of the door to climb up into the house.

The houses (*Naam*) were raised three to six feet above the ground level. The Nyishi did this to protect themselves from snakes and other ferocious wild animals. Some houses are also built slightly slanting into the hills to protect them from high winds and storms. The open space between the floor of the house and the ground was used to store *Assang* (fuel wood) and to shelter the poultry and pigs.

**Fig. 4: The *Naam*, a Typical Nyishi House.**

When harvesting trees and bamboo for house construction, the villagers strike them with the back of *uryuk* (a thick and flat iron-made sharp machete), an essential tool that is part and parcel of their everyday life. A metallic, ringing sound confirms the maturity of the trees. It was reported that the Nyishi harvested the tree species during the full moon days, i.e., between the last few days of the month and the first few days when there is less chance of degradation owing to termite attack.

### *Jhum (Shifting Cultivation): The Main Crop Production System*

Almost all members of the Nyishi community are peasants whose ancestors have used shifting cultivation from time immemorial. In practicing *Jhum* and other land uses, they apply indigenous knowledge ranging from selecting land to harvesting crops.

#### *Selection of Land for Jhum*

The Nyishi go to the hills in January to select a convenient piece of land for *Jhum*. The main task is to judge soil fertility through the vigour of secondary growth. To avoid conflict, the farmers would select the land for Jhum, which was not close to another farmer. They also take into consideration the maintenance of a wood and bamboo reserve for the use of members of a nearby hamlet.

#### *Land Preparation*:

Burning the bushes is an essential part of preparing the land for planting. The farmers burn their *Jhum* fields in the morning or evening when there is little wind to reduce the danger of the fire spreading to their houses. If the field to be burnt was very close to the hamlet, the farmers wait until it is dark so that lying sparks can be more easily seen. Farmers equipped with water pots, ladles, and banana leaves may be stationed on the roof of every house to protect them. After burning, the partially charred, larger logs in the *Jhum* land are placed across the field slope to reduce runoff and soil erosion.

#### *Seed Collection*:

The seeds of crops for successive *Jhum* are collected and set aside during the preceding harvest. Healthy ripened paddies are harvested separately, sun-dried in the open place (*Sar*) beside the dwelling house on the bamboo mats, and finally stored in *Nasung* (granary).

#### *Trees Left to Stand in Jhum Land*:

In earlier times, the Nyishi loved a neatly cleaned field, and they used to fell all the larger trees during land preparation in *Jhum*. Nowadays, they cut most of the trees and all bushes, leaving some fruit trees and leguminous species like *Pihak* (Soyabean, *Glycine max*) and *Piring* (Common Bean, *Phaseolus vulgaris*) on the assumption that the production of *Jhum* crops increased under these trees (Fig. 5).

**Fig. 5: A *Jhum* Field.**

### *The Farmers*

Irrespective of gender, the villagers spend their whole day from dawn to dusk in the *Jhum* land. They take their meal (mainly rice) together, wrapping it in fresh banana leaves to keep it warm. The use of banana leaves is extensive in the Nyishi community. They make the covers of water pots from fresh, folded leaves, store leafy vegetables wrapped in the leaves, and even serve food to the members of the family on them. Banana leaves have traditionally been used for such purposes worldwide – especially early among the Nyishis, where soybeans were wrapped in banana leaves and left out in the warm sun to ferment.

### *Manufacture of Plant-Based Household Utensils*

Woven baskets are an essential part and parcel of Nyishi's daily activities (Fig. 6). Every male member of the family was reported to weave baskets – a predominantly male task. Even women were also seen to be involved in basket making. Baskets vary in type, size, shape, and pattern according to their possible use. For instance, there are baskets for seed storage, others for retaining harvested crops, baskets for women, and others for men; there are portable baskets and stationary ones; baskets for clothing or chickens, and even for jewellery items and cosmetics. The baskets range from very small to very large, from delicate and lidded ones in which women generally keep their jewellery to woven baskets that transport cotton and fuel wood.

**Fig. 6: A Nyishi Man and Woman Making Baskets from Bamboo & Rattan/Cane, respectively.**

Baskets of many kinds were mainly made of bamboo (particularly *Bambusa vulgaris* and *Melocanna baccifera*) and rattans (e.g., *Calamus tenuis*). Carrying straps are generally made from the inner bark of trees obtained by beating the tree's trunk to remove the bark. Generally, all the ethnic communities residing in and around the forests in the Kurung Kumey district carry the baskets using a strap across the forehead. They need a smooth, comfortable strap that does not scratch or bruise their skin - as ropes or cords tend to do. The inner bark gives them the desired comfort and is abundant in hill forest areas. The farmers' success in identifying this material through trial and error reflects their intimate knowledge of the probable uses of the natural resources in the vicinity of their residence.

Among the everyday articles Nyishi uses, *Upum,* the storage pot for water, was found to be an interesting utensil. It was reportedly made from a gourd, which grows in the *Jhum* fields. The soft inside of these thick-bellied gourds is left to rot and then dried until only the hard shell remains; these are then used as water containers. Water was fetched from the surrounding *sang/kamcho* (natural springs) and hill streams in the *Upum* and drunk directly from them.

### *Management of Domestic Animals*

The domestic animals kept by the Nyishi are mainly chickens, cows, pigs, and goats. Among these, pigs are the most important. Pig keeping is not only a practice of the Nyishi. However, it is very common among all the tribal communities in Arunachal Pradesh, especially among the Tani group of tribes which includes Nyishi and other tribes, i.e., Adi, Apatani, Galo, and Tagin. They commonly slaughtered pigs as a sacrifice in various religious and spiritual ceremonies in the tribal society of the region. The farmers castrate male piglets. According to them, an uncastrated boar would not fatten up, and the meat would not taste good. Castration is done at the age of one to two months. The farmers reported that this early castration causes no problems since the boars are sexually mature soon after birth and suckle from the prostrate mother sow and copulate with her.

### *Processing Plant Raw Materials for Clothing*

The female members of Nyishi families weave their everyday attire themselves. They prepare the yarn from *Tachak-Sangne* (cotton-producing plants) in the *Jhum*. Barks of *Taking-Taming* (common madder or Indian madder, *Rubia cordifolia*) were soaked in water overnight in an earthen pot mixed with bamboo ashes. On the following day, the yarn and liquid are boiled together. After boiling, the yarns are hung up in the *Koda* (open space) of the dwelling house to facilitate drying. Repeating this procedure two to three times turns the yarns completely black. Some women also reported that in the earlier days, when there was a non-availability of yarns and clothes, they used to prepare yarns from a plant called *Pusu-Puyu* (Stinging nettle, *Urtica dioica*). However, these practices are hardly seen among very few families. With the modern ready-made clothes available, people felt like wasting time processing these indigenously made yarns and clothes.

**Fig. 7: A Nyishi Woman Carrying Basket as Head Load on the Way from Jhum.**

## Discussion

The perception and nature of indigenous knowledge of ethnic communities and local people vary from area to area. The use of forest plants as food by indigenous peoples throughout the world has been recorded by many authors (Banik, 1997; Maikhuri et al., 2000; Samal, 1997; Jana & Chauhan, 2000; Chandra, 2002; Idris & Mohamad, 2002; Renuka & Thomas, 2004; Shrestha & Dhillion, 2006; Uptrey et al., 2012; Murtem & Chaudhry, 2016; Jha, 2017; Lungphi et al., 2018; Asha & Singh, 2020; Hazarika & Tayeng, 2020; Eko et al., 2020; Gajurel & Doni, 2020; Hazarika et al., 2021). They noted that all depend largely on wild resources of plant and animal origin for food security.

The use of natural herbal drugs to alleviate suffering is an old indigenous medicine system worldwide (Mehrotra, 1989). From time immemorial, the hill people of Arunachal Pradesh have traditionally and culturally used plants to cure diseases and for aesthetic reasons. As discussed earlier, the Nyishi people reported using around 25 plant species as ethnomedicines for different ailments. People prefer wild to cultivated plants as a source of medicinal treatments.

Although *Jhum* (shifting cultivation) has become both environmentally and economically incompatible with the land use system due to the shortening of the fallow period caused by the government control over forests, legal restrictions on keeping land fallow for a long period, steadily increasing population pressure, and commercialisation of agriculture), remains the dominant land use type in the Kurung Kumey district region.

The IK of the Nyishi harnessed within the practice of *Jhum,* and their level of forest products consumption may provide some clues to maintaining the sustainability of the fragile ecosystem. Keeping wood and bamboo reserve for the community prior to land selection for *Jhum*, retaining leguminous trees in *Jhum* land, and placing partially charred logs across the hill slope to reduce soil erosion due to run-off ensures the sustainable management of hill resources.

Harvesting mature plants for construction, followed by treatment using indigenous methods, indirectly reduces the pressure on forest exploitation. Harvesting trees during the dry months is advantageous because tree growth is comparatively slower during the dry months due to low moisture content in the soil. So there is less starch content in the wood, making the wood less susceptible to insect and fungal attacks. Winter's low temperatures and humidity also reduce the likelihood of attack by other wood-deteriorating agents. Similarly, primarily using above-ground herbaceous plants and shrubs for food and medicine ensures the long-term viability of these forest resources.

## Conclusion

The preceding discussions of the study show that the Nyishi tribe is so dependent on forests that they are an integral component of the forest ecosystem. Many forest components are used in every aspect of life for survival and sustenance. These applications reflected their extensive indigenous knowledge (IK). The scientific community has increasingly recognised the value of farmers' IK in managing their natural resources over the last few decades. Indigenous knowledge (IK) plays an important role in managing forest resources and watersheds, as well as in conserving biodiversity and traditional cultural diversity. It serves as the foundation for the current agroforestry practice by Nyishi farmers in the Kurung Kumey district. It has the potential to contribute to the development of other improved systems in the future.

The IK-based practices of the Nyishi tribe ensure the sustenance of biological diversity that can become a key element in the sound management of forest resources. Therefore, scientific communities can play very useful roles in documenting these hereditary IKs and combining them with their scientific knowledge. Then, exploring better options for dual purposes - managing forest resources in mountain ecosystems and conserving indigenous wisdom as a part of living cultural-ecological systems. Furthermore, policymakers may gain some insights from the current study's findings in designing ethnicity-specific development projects, not only in the Kurung Kumey district but also in other parts of Arunachal Pradesh, that are compatible with the traditional beliefs of native inhabitants.

## References

Asha, H., & Singh, A.V. (2020). Diversity of medicinal wild fruits in the Lower Subansiri district of Arunachal Pradesh in Northeast India. *Asian Journal of Conservation Biology*, *9*(1), 113-122.

Atran, S. (1999). Managing the Maya commons: The value of local knowledge. In V.D. Nazarea (Ed.), *Ethno-ecology: Situated knowledge/located lives*. Tucson: University of Arizona Press.

Banik, R.L. (1997). The edibility of shoots of Bangladesh bamboos and their continuous harvesting effect on productivity. *Bangladesh Journal of Forest Science*, *26*(1), 1-10.

Chandra, V. (2002). Forest as source of wild edible plants for tribals. *Annals of Forestry*, *10*(1), 159-166.

Deb, S., Arunachalam, A., & Das, A.K. (2009). Indigenous knowledge of *Nyishi* tribes on traditional agroforestry systems. *Indian Journal of Traditional Knowledge*, *8*(1), 41-46.

Dwivedi, A.P. (1993). *Forest: The non-wood resources*. Dehradun: International Book Distributors.

Eko, R., Ngomle, S., Kanwat, M., Kalita, H., Moyon, N.N. (2020). Eating from the wild: An insight into the indigenous wild edible plants consumed by the Digaru Mishmi tribe of Arunachal Pradesh. *Indian Journal of Traditional Knowledge*, *19*(2), 360-369.

Gajurel, P.R., & Doni, T. (2020). Diversity of wild edible plants traditionally used by the Galo tribe of Indian Eastern Himalayan state of Arunachal Pradesh. *Plant Science Today*, *7*(4), 523–533. https://doi.org/10.14719/pst.2020.7.4.855.

Hazarika, P., Handique, C., & Hazarika, P. (2021). Documentation of edible plants in homesteads of Khampti tribe, Namsai district, Arunachal Pradesh, India. *International Journal of Advanced Research in Biological Sciences*, *8*(7), 64-80. DOI: http://dx.doi.org/10.22192/ijarbs.2021.08.07.008.

Hazarika, T., & Tayeng, B. (2020). Wild Edible Fruits of Arunachal Pradesh, India: Ethno-Medicinal Uses, Socio Economic Importance and Role in Rural Economy and Livelihood Security. PREPRINT (Version 2) available at Research Square https://doi.org/10.21203/rs.3.rs-51721/v2.

Idris, M.A.M., & Mohamad, A. (2002). Bamboo shoot utilisation in peninsular Malaysia: A case study in Pahang. *Journal of Bamboo and Rattan*, *1*(2), 141-155.

ILO (2019). Implementing the ILO indigenous and tribal peoples – Convention No. 169: Towards an inclusive, sustainable and just future. Geneva: ILO. https://www.ilo.org/global/publications/books/WCMS_735607/lang—en/index.htm

IWGIA (2020, May 11). Indigenous World 2020: India. https://www.iwgia.org/en/india/3601-iw-2020-india.html

Jana, S.K., & Chauhan, A.S. (2000). Ethno-botanical studies on *Lepchas* of *Dzongu*, North Sikkim, India. *Annals of Forestry*, *8*(1), 131-144.

Jha, K.K. (2017). Heritage non timber forest product use and management by indigenous community in Northeastern Himalayan hotspot, Arunachal Pradesh, India. *Journal of Plant Chemistry and Ecophysiology*, *2*(1), 1-12.

Larsen, P.B. (2000). Working with indigenous peoples in ecoregion conservation: further information. In *Indigenous and traditional peoples of the world and ecoregion conservation*. Gland, Switzerland: WWF.

Lungphi, P., Wangpan, T., & Sumpam, T. (2018). Wild edible plants and their additional uses by the Tangsa community living in the Changlang district of Arunachal Pradesh, India. *Pleione*, *12*(2), 151-164. https://doi.org/10.26679/Pleione.12.2.2018.151-164.

Maikhuri, R.K., Nautiyal, S., Rao, K.S., & Semwal, R.L. (2000). Indigenous knowledge of medicinal plants and wild edibles among three tribal subcommunities of the Central Himalayas, India. *Indigenous knowledge and Development Monitor*, *8*(2), 7-13.

Masreque, M.S., & Khan, N.A. (2000). Indigenous knowledge: A suitable strategy of sustainable development. *Grassroots Voice, 3*(1&2), 1–8.

Mehrotra, J.K. (1989). Collection and processing of plants for biological screening. In S.K. Jain (Ed.), *Methods and approaches in ethno-botany*. Lucknow: Society of Ethno-Botanists.

Murtem, G., & Chaudhry, P. (2016). An ethnobotanical note on wild edible plants of Upper Eastern Himalaya, India. *Brazilian Journal of Biological Sciences, 3*(5), 63-81. http://dx.doi.org/10.21472/bjbs.030506.

Negi, S.S. (1996). *Forests for socio-economic and rural development in India*. New Delhi: M.D. Publications Pvt. Ltd.

Oviedo, G., & Mafi, K. (2000). Toward a bio-cultural approach to conserving the diversity of life in the world's eco-regions. In *Indigenous and traditional peoples of the world and eco-region conservation*. Gland, Switzerland: WWF.

Pramukh, K.E.R. and Palkumar, P.D.S. (2006). Indigenous knowledge: implications in tribal health and disease. *Studies of Tribes and Tribals, 4*(1), 1–6.

Ramakrishnan, P.S. (1992). *Shifting agriculture and sustainable development: A interdisciplinary study from North-Eastern India*. Paris: UNESCO.

Ramakrishnan, P.S. (2007). Sustainable mountain development: The Himalayan tragedy. *Current Science, 92*(3), 308-316.

Ramakrishnan, P.S., Das, A.K. & Saxena, K.G. (eds.) (1996). *Conserving biodiversity for sustainable development*. New Delhi: Indian National Science Academy.

Ramakrishnan, P.S., Purohit, A.N., Saxena, K.G. & Rao, K.S. (1994). *Himalayan environment and sustainable development*. New Delhi: Indian National Science Academy.

Ramakrishnan, P.S., Saxena, K.G. & Chandrasekhara, U. (eds.) (1998). *Conserving the sacred: For biodiversity management*. New Delhi: Science Publishers.

Ramya, T. (2014a). Forest as a source of livelihood for the tribals of Kurung Kumey district, Arunachal Pradesh. In Manis Kumar Raha (Ed.), *North East India: The human landscape* (pp. 99-114). New Delhi: Concept Publishing Company Pvt. Ltd.

Ramya, T. (2014b). Natural resource utilisation among the Nyishi of Arunachal Pradesh: A reflection on the significance of indigenous knowledge systems. In K. Jose SVD & G.K. Bera (Eds.), *Indigenous resource management in North East India* (pp. 100-111). New Delhi: Omsons Publications.

Renuka, C., & Thomas, J.P. (2004). Rattan shoot – a tasty and nutritious food. *Evergreen – Half yearly Newsletter, No. 51 & 52*. Kerala Forest Research Institute, India.

Samal, J. (1997). Role of forest in a poor resource base tribal economy: A micro analysis. In P.M. Mohapatra & P.C. Mohapatro (Eds.), *Forest management in tribal areas*. New Delhi: Concept Publishing Company.

Shepherd, G. (1997). Trees on the farm and people in the forest: Social science perspectives in tropical forestry. *Commonwealth Forestry Review, 76*(1), 47–60.

Shrestha, M.P., & Dhillion, S.S. (2006). Diversity and traditional knowledge concerning wild food species in a locally managed forest in Nepal. *Agroforestry Systems, 66*(1), 55-63.

Singh, G.S. (2004). Indigenous knowledge and conservation practices in tribal society of Western Himalaya: A case study of Sangla Valley. *Studies of Tribes and Tribals*, *2*(1), 29–35.

Singh, L.R. (1997). *Social Foresty and forest development planning*. Delhi: Dey Publishing House.

Tripathi, A.K., Limasenla, & Shankar, R. (2017). Ethno-medicinal plants used by *Nyishi* tribe of Arunachal Pradesh, India. *World Journal of Pharmacy and Pharmaceutical Sciences*, *6*(5), 1246-1253.

Uprety, Y., Poudel, R.C., Shrestha, K.K., Rajbhandary, S., Tiwari, N.N., Shrestha, U.B., & Asselin, H. (2012). Diversity of use and local knowledge of wild edible plant resources in Nepal. *Journal of Ethnobiology Ethnomedicine*, *8*(16). https://doi.org/10.1186/1746-4269-8-16.

# 9

# In Defence of Indigeneity: Production of Health Practice among the Tea Tribes of Dooars

**Shima Saha, Ph.D & Dr T. Neishoning Koireng**

**Abstract**

Knowledge is produced as a result of interaction with the natural environment and maintained in a localised and traditional way of dealing with human life (UNESCO, 2020). The beginning of modernisation followed by the wave of globalisation has been a massive setback for the traditional belief system and practices prevalent among the indigenous people. The present paper proposes a study of the indigenous healing practices among the tea tribe community from the tea estates of Dooars regions of West Bengal. Efficacy of the local knowledge in healing practices is not only considered as stimuli but is also an alternative means to combat for survival. In tracing this trajectory, this paper tries to explain how the practices of such localised healing methods in the community are developing parallel to the model of sustainable development. This could be instrumental to the adaptive capabilities in the changing ecology of Dooars.

**Keywords:** Local Healing, Health, Indigenoues Knowledge, Tea Tribes, Adaptation, Sustainable Development.

## Introduction

People who are aboriginal to various places are believed to be the original natives of that place. Native people also termed as Indigenous people in specific areas, who have been assimilated, attached to nature and maintain their own way of life separate from the mainstream (Merlan, 2009). There are an estimated 370 million indigenous people in over 70 countries worldwide (Acabado, 2021). India as a country possesses great diversity in unity in its rich heritage. Census 2011 of India says, the tribal population of India is 8.6 percent of the total population of the country. Among this tribal population, particularly from Central India, including the Chhota-nagpur region of present-day Jharkhand state, tribal belts of Odisha, and tribal belts of Chhattisgarh were recruited as tea garden labourers or 'coolie' by the British colonial rulers (Sharma, 2009). In some parts of India, these labour communities are also recognised as 'Tea Tribes' (Borah, 2019). Whatever name this community is being called or recognised, they continue to imbibe their tradition, culture and knowledge system in various tea estates of India. Use of Indigenous knowledge in healing practices have been culturally accepted throughout human history and the evolution of the environment. Many tribal groups of India have been heavily reliant on the medicinal properties of plants for centuries. Such a form of practice has been an important part of culture and tradition. Tribal societies not only believe in using traditional medicines to treat a variety of diseases, but also preserve the knowledge, which is mostly passed orally down through generations. For healthcare, the native people depend upon medicinal herbs of their surroundings prescribed by local traditional healers (Sharma, 2005). Because of the high cost of modern medical care, the use of traditional herbal medicine for the treatment of common disorders has a lot of significance today among them.

Traditional knowledge of healing has been utilised by different ethnic groups or communities to treat a variety of diseases, but no records were kept. The present study found that the indigenous healing process has a significant impact on the Tea Tribe community (specially the Oraon, Munda and Kharia tribe) residing in New Lands Tea Garden of Alipurduar District of West Bengal. Therefore, there is a need to explore how the local traditional knowledge and practices has been carried out by the tea tribe community of Dooars. The study also aims to determine how such a knowledge system might aid in the alleviation of healthcare crisis and poverty among tea garden workers in line with the SDG paradigm (Sustainable development goal one and three).

## Study area

New Lands Tea Garden belongs to Dooars region of West Bengal. This tea garden is located in Kumargram Block of Alipurduar district in West Bengal, India. It is at the foothill of Bhutan hill Border, where the Raidak River and the Raidak forest is located. According to Alipurduar district survey report 2021, New Lands Tea Garden has a total population of 6,369 peoples (M-3147, F-3222) and the total geographical area of the village is 1154.7 hectares. There are about 1,315 houses in New Lands Tea

Garden. There are 1,545 permanent workers and an equal number of casual workers (non-permanent) in this tea garden.

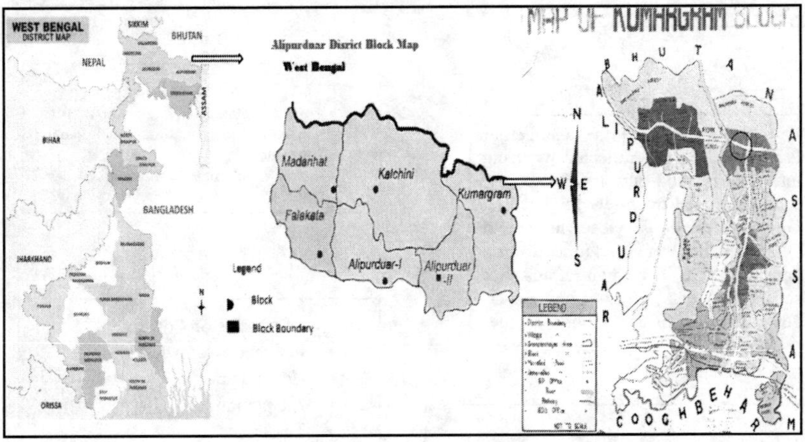


**Figure 1: Map of West Bengal, Alipurduar district and Kumargram block. (Source: Internet, BDO office Kumargram block)**

## Methodology

This study can be identified as an integral part of the author's PhD research work "Livelihood, Ecological Adaptation and Sustainability among the Tea Tribes: A Study on Tea plantations of Alipurduar District, West Bengal". Due to the outbreak of COVID-19, keeping the appropriate guidelines of it and with constraints of time and space, the data has been collected primarily from field surveys (2021). Tools included observation method, Focus Group Discussion (FGD) and interview method with open-ended questions from twenty Tribal community households of the New Lands Tea Garden. Also, data was collected from some secondary resources like local newspapers, government census reports, other researcher's books and journals.

## Findings

During field survey in the New Lands Tea Garden of Alipurduar district of West Bengal, it is found that this particular tea garden is near to Bhutan hills, surrounded by forest and water body. The place is enriched with a variety of flora and fauna. Tea tribes or the tea workers resided inside the tea estate. One permanent worker is allocated with a semi *pukka* house with tin shade roof but poorly maintained. Houses are arranged in a line known as *labour lines*, where there are separate houses for each family

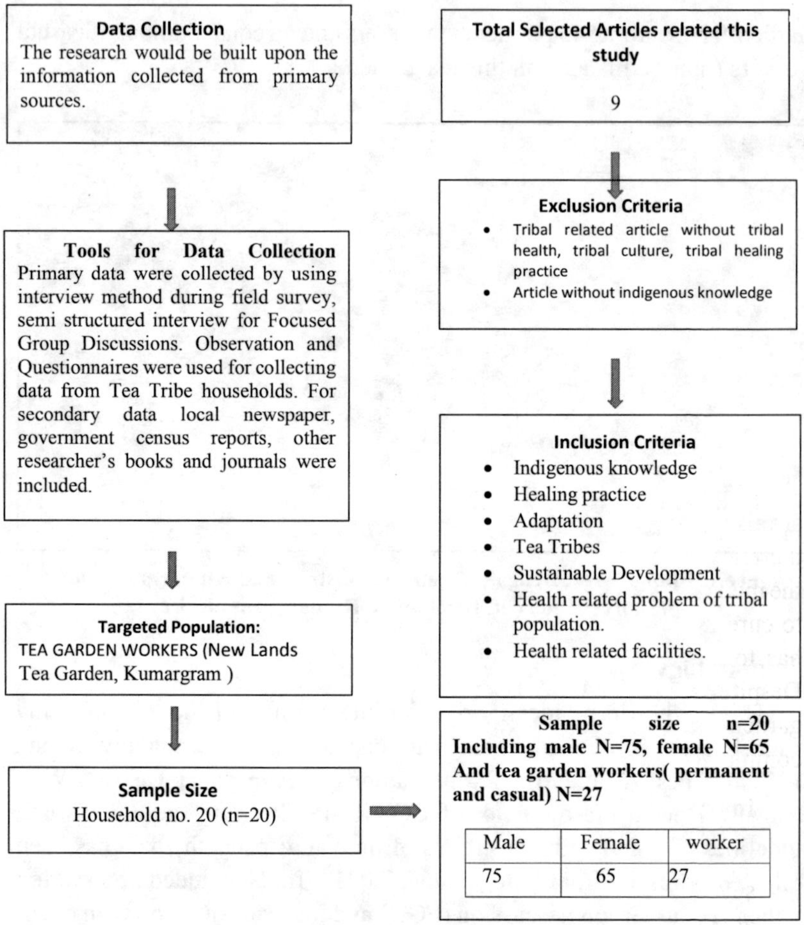


**Figure 2: Prisma Flow Chart of the Study.**

(Bhowmik,1996). Each family consists of more than five members. Out of it only one- or two-person work in the tea garden and the rest are children and retired old parents.

During FGD, a group of six female tea workers and four male workers stated that *"Essential commodity price of India is increasing day by day; it is very difficult for us to sustain our daily life depending on the minimum wage of Rs 202 per day, where it cannot meet the expenditures for all the family members including food, health and education needs."*

According to GNRTFN (Global Network for the Right to Food and Nutrition, 2016) report, there is a nutritionally unbalanced diet among the tea garden workers especially women throughout their life spans. The reason for malnutrition of diet to this group of women could be due to low income or due to low wages. Therefore, workers cannot afford balanced foods. Thus, nutritional well-being is not guaranteed as a prerequisite for workers to be healthy for work, raising their children, and learning and lead a healthy social life.

During FGD, the workers also said that-

> "To raise our economic status and nutritional well- being, we keep farm animals. As we believe that prices of essential commodities are high and vegetables are full of pesticides which are harmful for our health. Most of us are operating our own kitchen garden to survive from many difficult circumstances for our own well-being."

During the field visit, it was also found that indigenous healing practices are also prevalent among the Tea Tribe communities residing there. Although there is a hospital run by the tea estate authority (Bhowmik, 1996). Since the medical facilities provided there are poorly maintained, it lacks expertise to cure many diseases. As tea gardens are located in remote areas, if one has to avail advanced medical facilities it becomes very unaffordable. Despite being facilitated with advanced medical facilities within the tea garden, indigenous healing practices are popularly acceptable by the tribal communities residing in the garden in order to combat for survival.

In this respect one family from the labour line said that

> "Very often, we encounter wild snakes in the tea garden. There are several cases of snake bites as well as other poisonous insect bites, and attacks of elephants. During such horrific conditions, the tea garden management somehow provides an ambulance to avail treatment in the nearest healthcare center, which is far from the tea garden."

As per the opinion of people from the Tea Tribe community, it is observed that most of the tribal population has a strong belief in the local healing knowledge system. For them it is more affordable and they find it very convenient to visit the local healers. Most of the Tribal women prefer herbal treatments. With the help of their local indigenous knowledge that has been transmitted orally from their past generations, they could inculcate for certain healings.

A female Tea worker acknowledges that

> "Whenever I feel sick, I first opt for the remedies that I learned from my grandmother, mother and mother-in-law. We use such remedies

very often because the cost of medicines prescribed by the tea garden hospital doctors are expensive and not accessible at all times".

The ailments such as fever, cough, cold, high blood pressure, skin diseases and Jaundice are very common among the Tea Tribes. For such illnesses, they prefer herbal treatment, which they have obtained from the traditional knowledge system, over advanced medicine.

One women tea worker said that

"Cuts and wounds are very common while working in the tea garden. We rub green tea leaves on the wounds for quick healing. Ointments are very costly and not always accessible."

Thus, all the above statements collected from the tea garden during the field survey suggests that the poor economic condition could be one of the main reasons that compelled them to solely depend on natural resources from the ecology to meet their primary needs. They stack firewood to cook; collect varieties of foods from the jungle such as berries, edible leaves and livestock for food. Moreover, they collect and preserve herbal plants, what they consider as medicinal plants for both humans and their livestock. Another reason could be they valued natural resources which provide them freely in their ecology. It would not be wrong if we say indigenous or tribal people are protectors of nature.

List of some useful, easily accessible medicinal plants (leaves/roots/ stems) used by Tea Tribes living in New Lands tea garden are as follows:

- *Teetapatta* or bitter leaves which is found everywhere in the labour line. Fluid from these leaves is extracted and orally consumed. It is beneficial in controlling high blood pressure. It is also helpful for digestion system, controlling fever and healing wounds of humans as well as cattles.
- *Cuscuta* plant is consumed for quick relief from jaundice.
- *Vasaka or Basak (*scientific *name:* Justicia adhatoda) leaves and flowers for the treatment of respiratory ailments.
- *Tulsi* or Basil (scientific name: Ocimum basilicum) used for the treatment of common cough and cold.
- *Neem (*scientific name: Azadirachta indica) used for wide applications to the skin borne diseases. Also, Neem leaves used for natural pest control.

## Discussion

In the tea gardens of Assam and West Bengal, tea workers are not paid adequately compared their hard labour (Borah, 2017). Shelter is an essential need of human life perspective and it has been established standard living wellbeing (Das, 2021). The amount paid to workers as a wage is very low to live a standard life. This is because the prices of food and other necessity amenities are swelling up day by day in our country. The study found that the usage of indigenous healing systems over advanced health systems is more prevalent among the Tea Tribes in the tea gardens of the Alipurduar district, West Bengal. For the Tea Tribes, such knowledge plays a very significant role in their community. They desire to disseminate such knowledge of healing practices to others who are in need too. As various communities are closely inhabited amidst nature, they can also use this opportunity by utilising their knowledge to cure ailments (Mahant, 2015). Tea Tribe folks use various plants, which are available in their ecology, in their subconscious indigeneity for curing various ailments for their primary healthcare. Using of advanced medicines parallel to herbal treatment and belief systems of indigenous knowledge for curing day-to-day ailments is significant impact on modernisation (Dutta, 2014).

The condition of the Tea Tribe in the tea garden seems to be pathetic and painful. Changing Climate and change in weather patterns have a great impact on their lives too. Routinely, they work daily for eight to nine long hours standing in the midst of tea plantation plucking leaves. They work under the scorching sun in summer; under heavy rains during monsoon and cold shivering weather in winter. Notably, the worker seems to suffer most during the rainy season and winter. In addition, with the increasing population, they face scarcity of water. As a result, they end up in confrontation and fight among themselves. Poor infrastructure of their home and minimal wage adds to their misery. In each family unemployed outnumber the employed; although, some are in search of other modes of income or some are unable to work due to age factor. Some lack proper skills, qualifications, and various shortcomings, so they are helpless. Most of the men folk of the family migrate to other places to earn to support their family members (Sonar, 2018). Thus, poverty is prevailing among the tea tribes.

A central task of sustainable development is to mitigate extreme poverty in all its forms, promoting economic development and health for all. With the coming generation, i.e., by 2030, it should be possible to attain that all households have the access to basic needs through sufficient household income, decent nutrition, food security, and universal access to primary health services. Likewise, they get support for early childhood development, proper education for professional skills. Further, providing basic infrastructure to access services including safe water and sanitation, clean energy, and broadband connectivity.

The policy-maker should uphold the indigenous knowledge system in healing practice and solve many problems faced by tea tribes like the low wages, lack of health facility, ensuring nutritional well-being, healthy shelter, guidance etc. If these things are taken care of, it may improve the local ecology which may add to the sustainable livelihood of the tea garden workers. It may also help in reducing poverty to the model of sustainable development, and may achieve a better situation in economic and ecological benefits.

## Conclusion

Although various studies have been conducted in various tea gardens of Dooars, this particular study tries to highlight the importance of traditional knowledge in healing practices prevailing among the Tea Tribes. Such knowledge is helping them to cope up with the challenges due to poor economic conditions and poor healthcare facilities. Using observation and interview methodologies in the field, we discovered that their indigenous knowledge of medicinal plants for healing purposes is significant to their culture, economy, and well-being. As a result, there is a need for documenting and appraisal of knowledge that has been transmitted orally and may be lost in the near future. Thus, this study concludes that the ecological adaptation through the indigenous knowledge system and local indigenous healing practices put a positive impact on society. It has been realised that the importance of indigenous knowledge is going to play an important role in future for achieving the sustainable development goal.

## References

A Life without dignity –the price of your cup of tea, 2016, Global Network for the Right to Food and Nutrition,

https://www.righttofoodandnutrition.org/files/IndiaFFMReport_June_2016.pdf.

Bhowmik, S. (1996). *Tea plantation labour in India*. New Delhi.

Bhowmik, S. (1981). *Class formation in the plantation system*. People's Publishing House.

Borah, P. (2017). Tea Garden Labour Situation in Assam. *Sch. J. Arts Humanit. Soc.* Sci., 5(8C):985-989 DOI: 10.21276/sjahss.

Census Report of 2011.

Chatterjee, Subhasish, and Rahul Sharma. 2018. Belief of tribal's in supernatural power and its relation with religious life (with special reference to Indian tribal society). *International Journal of Research and Analytical Reviews 5:* 48–55.

Datta, T., Patra, A. K., & Dastidar, S. G. (2014). Medicinal plants used by tribal population of Coochbehar district, West Bengal, India-an ethnobotanical survey. *Asian Pacific journal of tropical biomedicine,* 4(Suppl 1), S478–S482.

https://doi.org/10.12980/APJTB.4.2014C1122.

https://www.iosrjournals.org./iosr-jhss/papers/Vol20-issue1/Version- 1/ H020114954.pdf.

Mahant, SD (2015). Indigenous Traditional Healing Care: Belief & Practices among Tribals of South Bastar in Chhattisgarh, *IOSR Journal Of Humanities And Social Science, 20(1)*, 49-54, DOI:10.9790/0837-20114954

Merlan, F. (2009). Indigeneity: Global and Local. *Current Anthropology, 50(3),* 303-333. https://doi.org/10.1086/597667., https://www.jstor.org/stable/10.1086/ 597667.

Report of the UNESCO Expert Meeting on Indigenous Knowledge and Climate Change in Africa-nairobi, Kenya. 27-28 June 2018, 2020 Report of the UNESCO Expert Meeting on Indigenous Knowledge and Climate Change in Africa, Nairobi, Kenya, 27-28 June 2018-UNESCO Digital Library.

SDG Indicators - Global indicator framework for the Sustainable Development Goals and targets of the 2030 Agenda for Sustainable Development. United Nation Statistics Division (UNSD). Retrieved 6 August 2020.

Sharma, J. (2009). "Lazy" Natives, Coolie Labour, and the Assam Tea Industry. *Modern Asian Studies, 43(6),* 1287–1324. http://www.jstor.org/stable/40285014.

Sonar, A. et., al. (2018). Migration and livelihood of Dooars tea garden: case study of Chinchula tea estate, Alipurduar district, North Bengal. *IJMR, 4(9):* 77-84.

Sustainable Development goals, Department of Economic and Social Affairs, https://sdgs.un.org/goals

Uday Das, and Dr. Rafiqul Islam. (2021). Livelihood Realism: A Review on Closed Tea Gardens of Dooars, West Bengal. *International Journal of Research Granthaalayah, 9(2),* 72-80.https://doi.org/10.29121/granthaalayah. v9.i2.2021.3355

# 10

# Ethnomedicinal Practices of the Angami Nagas of Viphoma Village of Kohima District, Nagaland

**Ketousieno Kuotsuo**

## Introduction

Ethnomedicine is the study of ethnography of health and healing behaviours in various societies. It encompasses methods of diagnosis and treatment (Bhasin, 2007). Ethnomedicine helps us to understand the health practices of various indigenous communities. Further, it provides deeper insights into the people's world view and indigenous knowledge systems regarding diagnosis and therapeutic practices. The word 'ethnomedicine' is sometimes used as a synonym for traditional medicine (Acharya and Srivastava, 2008) or indigenous medicine or folk medicine. Since the time of the non-existence of the modern healthcare system, people from these societies had been living under the protection of traditional medicines collected from their habitat premises and the forests in their vicinity (Mwchahary and Nath, 2015). Traditional medicine has been providing primary healthcare to almost 80 percent of the world's population (Mukherji, 2002; Alves and Rosa, 2005) and has been playing a significant role in the healthcare system (Islam, 2009).

The state of Nagaland situated in the North-Eastern region of India has a valuable heritage of ethnomedicinal knowledge. Every Naga community has developed their traditional ways of diagnosing and treating certain kinds of diseases. The wealth of this information is preserved as an unwritten Materia Medica of this tribal folk (Pfoze and Chiezou, 2006). The Angami, like any other Naga tribe, depends on their ethnomedicine when contracted by illnesses. Certain age-old healing techniques for different illnesses are practiced; especially those residing in remote areas where access to modern medicine remains a challenge. Considering that, Viphoma village has been selected for the study and an account of their ethnomedicinal practices is explored.

## The study area – Viphoma Village

Viphoma Village is a remote Angami village located 41 km away from Kohima, Nagaland. The village covers an area of about 14 sq.km. Neighbouring villages are Zhadima, Phekerkriema, Tsiepama and Menguzouma. The total number of households in the village is 116 with a total population of 489, out of which 245 are male and 244 are female.

The village is divided into three khels based on their locality: Chazou Khel (upper), Ketsuoki Khel (middle) and Chakou Khel (lower). To maintain peace and solidarity among the village members and to effectively administer the affairs of the village, the day-to-day administration is controlled by the Village Chairman along with the council members.

As far as the amenities are concerned, almost all the houses are electrified. The supply of water remains poor and thus, the villagers face water scarcity during the dry season. They practice rainwater harvesting for water conservation. However, rainwater alone is not sufficient to meet their daily requirements throughout the year. Concerning medical facilities, a rudimentary dispensary exists in the village where first aid can be availed. Medicines for common ailments like fever, cough and cold can be availed but the irregularity of medical supply hampers the smooth functioning of the dispensary.

## Ethnomedicinal Practices

In the absence of proper healthcare facilities in the village, the people cope with health problems by applying their knowledge on the use of different types of medicinal plants, animal products and other items available within their reach.

Most healthcare takes place in the home either self-administered or given by members of the family. Oftentimes, the mother of the household manages taking care of the children's ailments. Generally, the elders provide treatment when any member of the family suffers from an illness. People normally keep first aid kits and medicine like paracetamol in their house for common illnesses such as colds, fever, abdominal pains, etc. For minor ailments like cold and cough, people generally treat themselves by preventing chilling or drinking chicken soup. One of the most popular examples of a home remedy seen in many households is providing chicken soup or pork leg soup for regaining strength in times of weakness. Other ingredients like ginger and honey mixed with warm water or massaging warm mustard oil mixed with garlic are used to treat or provide relief from common illnesses like cough, sore throat, stomachache, etc. Honey (*mepfi dzii*) is also a commonly available item in every kitchen which is often used as a medicine for gastric problems. It has also been observed that doing self-treatment with medicinal plants found in the locality is very common. A good number of plants and animals are used extensively for treating a variety of health problems.

## Use of plants as medicine

In Angami's terminology, the word *"nhadaru"* refers to medicinal plants. The knowledge on the use of medicinal plants for curing different illnesses is known to many village members especially by the older generation. A total of 70 medicinal plants from the village have been identified and documented below.

**Table 1: Medicinal plants and their mode of application**

| Sl. No. | Botanical name | Family | Vernacular name/ Common name | Uses |
|---|---|---|---|---|
| 1. | *Ageratum conyzoides* | *Asteraceae* | *Tephrienha/* Chickweed | Leaves are ground and applied oncuts and wounds for blood clotting. |
| 2. | *Allium chinense* | *Amaryllidaceae* | *Khuvie/* Japanese scallion | The bulb and leaves help in reducing cholesterol level in the blood. |
| 3. | *Allium hookeri* | *Amaryllidaceae* | *Siila/* Garlic chives | The leaves are eaten cooked orraw for deworming. |
| 4. | *Allium sativum* | *Amaryllidaceae* | *Chiimerie/* Garlic | The bulb is sliced and inhaled to stop nose bleeding. The bulb is also eaten raw for lowering high B.P. |
| 5. | *Alnus nepalensis* | *Betulaceae* | *Riipruo/* Indian Alder | Leaves are ground and paste is applied to the affected parts of the body for allergy. Leaf extract is also applied to the body for body ache and weakness. |
| 6. | *Aloevera* | *Asphodelaceae* | *Aloevera* | Eaten raw to get relief from gastric problems. It is also applied to burns and scars. |
| 7. | *Artimisia nilagirica* | *Asteraceae* | *Chena/* Wormwood | Leaves are crushed and inserted into the nostrils to stop nose bleeding. |

| Sl. No. | Botanical name | Family | Vernacular name/Common name | Uses |
|---|---|---|---|---|
| 8. | *Asparagus officinalis* | *Asperagaceae* | *Shieprii/* Asparagus | The stem is cooked and eaten to cure high B.P. and urinary infections. Also effective in preventing the formation of kidney stones. |
| 9. | *Auriculariales* | *Auriculariaceae* | *Temyiinuonye/* Wood ear, jelly ear | The jelly-like mushroom is used as a plaster over injured wounds. |
| 10. | *Averrhoa carambola* | *Oxalidaceae* | *Starfruit* | The fruit is eaten to cure jaundice. |
| 11. | *Azadirachtaindica* | *Meliaceae* | *Khusia/* Neem | The fruit is immersed in water and is used as a medicine for high BP, fever and also drunk to cure a hangover. The leaves are boiledin water and drank to cure fever. |
| 12. | *Bambuseae* | *Poaceae* | *Kerie/* Bamboo | The bark is scraped and used for covering injured wounds. Young shoots are also eaten for stomach disorders. |
| 13. | *Capsicum chinense* | *Solanaceae* | *Raza/* Naga king chilli | The fruit is taken in small quantities for cold and flu. It also aids in weight loss and diabetes. |
| 14. | *Carica* | *Caricaceae* | *Kopita/* Papaya | The fruit is eaten for gastric problems and constipation. |
| 15. | *Centellaasiatica* | *Apiaceae* | *Gara/* Indian pennywort | The whole plant is boiled in water or eaten raw to cure gastric problems. |
| 16. | *Cheilocostus speciosus* | *Costaceae* | *Lhouchiegavanyii/* Crepe ginger | Leaves boiled in water are drankfor kidney stones. |
| 17. | *Chenopodium album* | *Amaranthaceae* | *Tsonha/* Wild spinach | Leaves are crushed and paste isapplied on white patches on the skin. |
| 18. | *Cinnamomum verum* | *Lauraceae* | *Seichii/* Cinnamon | The bark is used as a condiment in curry for its anti-diabetic effect. It also improves digestion and helps reduce B.P. |
| 19. | *Citrus* | *Rutaceae* | *Siihuo/* Lemon | The juice is squeezed and used against cold, cough, headache and indigestion. It is also rubbed on the forehead to get relief from headaches. |
| 20. | *Citrus maxima* | *Rutaceae* | *Siihuo hulo/* Pomelo | The peel of the fruit is soaked in water and drunk to cure diabetes. |
| 21. | *Colocasia esculenta* | *Araceae* | *Dziinuo/* Taro | The stem/ stalk of the plant is used in incidences of insect or snake bites. The spongy stalk absorbs the venom from a snake bite when applied over the wound. |
| 22. | *Cucumissativus* | *Cucurbitaceae* | *Tsiituo/* Cucumber | Juice of fermented fruit is drunkfor gastric problems. |

| Sl. No | Botanical name | Family | Vernacular name/ Common name | Uses |
|---|---|---|---|---|
| 23. | *Curculigo crassifolia* | *Hypoxidaceae* | *Chage nyii/ thage nyii/* Palm grass | The root is sliced and soaked in water and drunk to cure gastric problems. The root is also boiled and drunk for jaundice. |
| 24. | *Cyphomandra betacea* | *Solanaceae* | *Sei benganuo/* Tree tomato | The fruit is eaten raw for blood cleansing. It also helps to cure migraines and headaches. |
| 25. | *Dolichos lablab* | *Fabaceae* | *Riitsii/* Hyacinth bean | The root boiled in water is drunk for abdominal pain. |
| 26. | *Drymaria cordata* | *Caryophy-llaceae* | *Pfii pfii nyii/* Chick weed | Leaf paste is applied as a thincoat over boils for easy removal of pus from boils. Leaves are also burnt and inhaled to get relief from sinus problems. |
| 27. | *Elatosterma lineolatum* | *Urticaceae* | *Gadzo* | Leaves are cooked and eaten for purifying blood and also for gastrointestinal problems. |
| 28. | *Elscholtzia blanda* | *Lamiaceae* | *Nyienhyii/* Pleasant Himalayan mint | Dried flowers and leaves are taken with salt to cure nausea. It is used in the treatment of kidney and urinary problems. |
| 29. | *Elscholtzia stauntonii* | *Lamiaceae* | *Khromhii/* Mint bush | The stomach is gently massaged with leaf paste to get relief from stomach aches. It is also boiled and drunk for headaches. |
| 30. | *Emblica officinalis* | *Phyllanthaceae* | *Chihusi/* Gooseberry | The fruit is used against coughs, colds and eye inflammation. |
| 31. | *Equisetum arvense* | *Equisetaceae* | *Shiihie/riizie nha/* Horsetail | The whole plant is finely chopped and infused in boiling water and drunk by a person who has kidney problems and has difficulty in passing urine. The juice is also drunk for curing arthritis and rheumatism. |
| 32. | *Eryngium foetidum* | *Apiaceae* | *Local dhania/* Burmese corriander | Leaves are consumed for curing jaundice. |
| 33. | *Eucalyptus* | *Myrtaceae* | *Vicks bo/* Eucalyptus | Leaves are boiled in water andthe steam is inhaled for fever and malaria. |
| 34. | *Eupatorium adinophorum* | *Asteraceae* | *Japan nha/* Crofton weed | Leaves are ground and juice extract is drunk to cure diarrhoea. |
| 35. | *Fagopyrum tartaricum* | *Polygonaceae* | *Garei/* Tartary buckwheat | The leaves are boiled and eaten for curing high B.P. and diarrhoea. |
| 36. | *Ficus auriculata* | *Moraceae* | *Khabvii/* Elephant ear fig | The fruit is eaten for diabetes and the treatment of dysentery. |
| 37. | *Ficus semicordata* | *Moraceae* | *Chiede/* Drooping fig | Raw fruit is boiled and drank to cure high B.P. The fruit is also eaten to cure dysentery. |

| Sl. No | Botanical name | Family | Vernacular name/ Common name | Uses |
|---|---|---|---|---|
| 38. | *Glycine max* | *Fabaceae* | *Siidza/* Soyabean | Seeds are cooked and eaten which provide energy andstrength to the body during weakness. |
| 39. | *Gynura nepalensis* | *Asteraceae* | *Liezienuo* | Leaves are boiled and taken tocure constipation and stomach disorders. |
| 40. | *Hibiscus sabdariffa* | *Malvaceae* | *Gakhro/* Rozelle hemp | The leaves and flowers are taken for high B.P, increased passing of urine and also helps in weight management. |
| 41. | *Houttuynia cordata* | *Saururaceae* | *Gatha/* Fish mint, rainbow plant | Leaves are eaten raw to cleanse the blood. It also relieves stomach ache. |
| 42. | *Impatiens tripetala* | *Balsaminaceae* | *Gapfii* | Leaves are boiled and either drunk or eaten for gastric problems and constipation. |
| 43. | *Mentha spicata* | *Lamiaceae* | *Pudina/* Spearmint | Leaves are boiled in water and taken to cure gastric problems. Raw leaves are eaten to cure pneumonia, gallstone problem, vomiting, toothache. Leaf paste is also applied on joints or massa-ged on the body for body ache. |
| 44. | *Mimosa pudica* | *Fabaceae* | *Nha menga/* Touch me not | Roots and leaves are boiled and taken for treating pile problems, diarrhoea and skin problems. |
| 45. | *Mirabilisjalapa* | *Nyetaginaceae* | *Kebal nye/* 4 o'clock plant | Leaves crushed and applied onte nostril checks nose bleeding. |
| 46. | *Momordica charantia* | *Cucurbitaceae* | *Keriela/* Bitter gourd | The fruit is cooked and consumed for diabetes and also for expelling worms. |
| 47. | *Musa paradisiaca* | *Musaceae* | *Thayie* (fruit) *Tepfhe* (stem)/ Banana | Juice collected from the stem is drunk to cure dysentery. The fruit is also eaten for dysentery. |
| 48. | *Ocimum tenuiflorum* | *Lamiaceae* | *Nyiechu/* Basil | Leaves are boiled in water and taken to lower high blood pressure and diabetes. Also used as a medicine for cough. |
| 49. | *Oenanthe javanica* | *Apiaceae* | *Gakra/* Water celery, Chinese celery | Leaves are boiled and eaten toget relief from gastritis. |
| 50. | *Oroxylum indicum* | *Bignoniaceae* | *Priza/* Trumper flower | The bark of the tree is scraped and a paste is prepared for covering wounds and broken bones. The bark is also boiled in water and drank for the properfunctioning of the liver. |
| 51. | *Paris polyphylla* | *Melanthiaceae* | *Tinhyiimiadzii/* Herb paris | The root is boiled in water and drunk to cure kidney problems. |
| 52. | *Parkia timoriana* | *Fabaceae* | *Tepfi riitsii/* Tree bean | Beans either raw or cooked are eaten to prevent constipation. It is also known to have anti-cancer properties. |

| Sl. No | Botanical name | Family | Vernacular name/ Common name | Uses |
|---|---|---|---|---|
| 53. | *Passiflora edulis* | *Passifloraceae* | *Bel/* Passion fruit | Leaves are boiled in water and drunk to lower high blood pressure. |
| 54. | *Plantago asiatica* | *Plantaginaceae* | *Gapa/* Chinese plantain | Leaves are boiled in water and drank to lower high B.P., also cures constipation. |
| 55. | *Polygonum chinense* | *Polygonaceae* | *Gazhie/* Chinese knotwood | Leaves are boiled in water and drunk to cure diabetes and high B.P. |
| 56. | *Psidium guajava* | *Myrtaceae* | *Moduram/* Guava | Leaves are chewed raw to cure dysentery. |
| 57. | *Punica granatum* | *Lythraceae* | *Touram/* Pomegranate | Leaves boiled in water is drunk to cure pneumonia, fever and malaria. The fruit is also consumed by diabetic patients. |
| 58. | *Rhus semialata* | *Anacardiaceae* | *Zomhu/*Chinese gall, nutgall | The fruit is mashed and powdered and is taken for headache, stomachache, dysentery, indigestion, vomiting and food poisoning. |
| 59. | *Ricinus communis* | *Euphorbiaceae* | *Sopfii tekhrie/lukha/* Castor bean | The leaves are heated over the fire and placed on joints to get relief from arthritis *(meii).* |
| 60. | *Rubus ellipticus* | *Rosaceae* | *Ruomvii/* Wild raspberry | The fruit is soaked in water and drunk to cure jaundice. The juice of the fruit is also used in the treatment of fever, cough and sore throat. |
| 61. | *Saccharum officinarum* | *Poaceae* | *Meke/* Sugarcane | Juice is drunk to cure jaundice and gall bladder problems. It is also used as an ear drop. |
| 62. | *Sechium edule* | *Cucurbitaceae* | *Squash/* Chayote | Young tender fruit is eaten raw tocure gastric problems. It is also known to have anti-ageing properties. |
| 63. | *Solanum indicum* | *Solanaceae* | *Sipfii si/* African egg plant | The fruit is mashed and mixed with water and drunk for curing cough. |
| 64. | *Solanum khasianum* | *Solanaceae* | *Porpo/* Nightshade | The fruit is burnt and smoke is applied inside the mouth to get relief from toothache. |
| 65. | *Solanum lycopersicum* | *Solanaceae* | *Kero benganuo/* Garden tomato | Fruit crushed and applied on the scalp promotes hair growth. It also helps with skin irritation. |
| 66. | *Spilanthes acmella* | *Asteraceae* | *Kevenha/* Toothache plant | The flower is inserted inside the tooth cavity which gives relief from toothache. |
| 67. | *Tagetes erecta* | *Asteraceae* | *Phul/* Marigold | Juice extract of the leaf is used to cure a cough or sore throat in infants. |

| Sl. No | Botanical name | Family | Vernacular name/ Common name | Uses |
|---|---|---|---|---|
| 68. | *Xanthoxylu marmatum* | *Rutaceae* | *Temyii ganya/* Winged prickly-ash | Leaves are ground and juice extract is taken to cure pneumonia. Leaf paste is also smeared and massaged on the body to cure pneumonia. Leaves and fruit are boiled and drunk to cure gas form. Leaf paste is also massaged on the belly for curing gas form. |
| 69. | *Zea mays* | *Poaceae* | *Siiko/* Maize | Consumption of corn either boiled or roasted is good for hypertension. It also helps in the production of breast milk. |
| 70. | *Zingiber officinale* | *Zingiberaceae* | *Kevii viichii/* Ginger | The rhizome is either crushed and applied for allergy or is mixed with warm water or honey andused as a medicine to cure cough. |

*Source:* Fieldwork.

**(I) *Mimosa pudica (Nha menga)***

**(II) *Impatiens tripetala (Gapfii)***

**(III) Xanthoxylum armatum (Temyii ganya)**

**(IV) Cheilocostus speciosus (Lhouchiegavanyii)**

**(V) Oenanthe javanica (Gakra)**

**(VI) Houttuynia cordata (Gatha)**

(*Source:* Fieldwork)

**(VII) Drymaria cordata (Pfii pfii nyii)**

**(VIII) Spilanthes acmella (Kevenha)**

**(IX) Polygonum chinense (Gazhie)**

**(X) Tagetes erecta (Phul)**

**(XI) Ficus semicordata (Chiede)**

**(XII) Rubus ellipticus (Ruomvii)**

*Source:* Fieldwork

**(XIII) Benincasa hipsida (Mengu)**

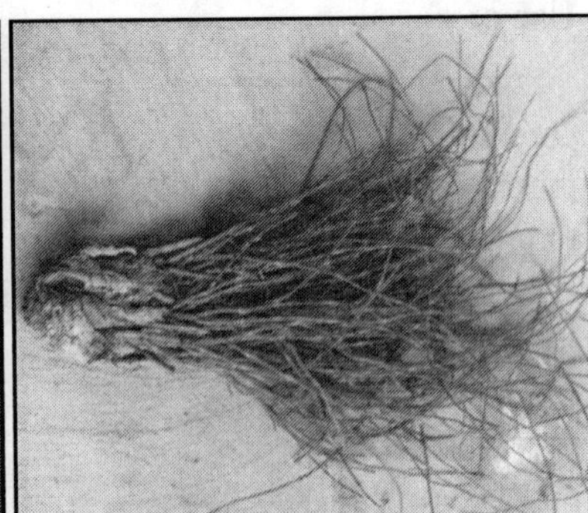

**(XIV) Equisetum arvense (Shiihie)**

**(XV) Auriculariales (Temyiinuonye)**

**(XVI) Paris polyphyla (Tinhyiimiadzii**

**(XVII): Colocasia esculenta (Dziinuo)**

**(XVIII): Solanum khasianum (Sokibohu)**

*Source:* Fieldwork

## Use of animal products

Animals and their by-products have been used in several ways by the people to get relief from certain illnesses. The table given below highlights the different types of animals and birds and their use which has been reported to provide desired healing in various kinds of illnesses.

**Table 2: Animals/birds and their medicinal uses**

| Sl.No. | Common name | Local name | Uses |
|---|---|---|---|
| 1. | Bat | *Siilhe* | The feather is considered medicinal and is used for covering burnt skin for quick recovery. |
| 2. | Bear | *Thega* | The bile is mixed with water and drunk for stomach pain, fever, body ache and sore eyes. |

| | | | |
|---|---|---|---|
| 3. | Cat | *Monyinuo* | The flesh is cooked and eaten for relieving asthma-related problems. |
| 4. | Chinese pangolin | *Tophu* | The scale of the animal has a medicinal property known to cure piles. The scale is tied with thread and is worn around the neck which cures piles. |
| 5. | Crab | *Siiguo* | Raw crab is ground and juice extract is consumed for curing cough and jaundice. |
| 6. | Deer | *Chiizie* | Urine is used as an ear drop to cure ear - problems.The fresh warm blood of the animal is collected and consumed to cure high B.P. Leg soup also facilitates delivery. |
| 7. | Dog | *Tepfii* | The flesh is cooked and consumed during weakness. Flesh soup improves pre and postpartum health. |
| 8. | Frog | *Guoriinuo* | The flesh is cooked and eaten after surgery for quick recovery of wounds. Skin is applied on burnt wounds for rapid healing. |
| 9. | Earthworm | *Zotshii* | Earthworm found in a banana stem is ground and juice is extracted. This juice serves as an antidote for snake bites. |
| 10. | Eel fish | *Tinhyii khuo* | Fresh blood is drunk to cure general weakness and to relieve anemia and asthma. |
| 11. | Goat | *Temyii* | Milk is drunk to during body weakness. Meat is also good for arthritis. |
| 12. | Lab rat | *Thezu kekra* | The meat of the animal is cooked and consumed for curing cough and pneumonia in children. |
| 13. | Mithun | *Gwi* | Mithun is sacrificed during important festivals. The male organ is cooked and eaten to relieve severe pain in the breast of a lactating mother. |
| 14. | Monkey | *Tepfi* | The bile is mixed with water and is taken as a medicine to cure cough. |
| 15. | Otter | *Khuorha* | The palm of the animal is used to massage the neck to remove fish bones that get stuck in the throat. |
| 16. | Pig | *Thevo* | Meat and soup are consumed during weakness. |
| 17. | Pila globosa | *Nula* | The flesh is eaten after cooking as a relief measure in asthma, tuberculosis, stomach disorders and eye-related problems. |

| | | | |
|---|---|---|---|
| 18. | Pigeon | *Barunuo* | Meat is cooked and eaten for general weakness. |
| 19. | Porcupine | *Chiekru* | The whole stomach along with the contents is boiled in water and drunk to cure fever and malaria.Fat is applied to relieve body ache, rheumatic pain, burning wounds and rapid healing of fractured bones. A small portion of the intestine is dried and then dipped overnight in cold water. This water is then drunk to cure cholera, dysentery and stomach disorders. It also aids in the delivery during childbirth. |
| 20. | Python | *Cie* | The fat is massaged on the body for body ache or backache. It is also applied to ringworms. The bile is also mixed with water and used as medicine. |
| 21. | Rat | *Zuthie* | The fresh blood of the animal is applied on scars and blemishes. |
| 22. | Serow | *Thelu* | The marrow (*keli*) is applied to fractured bones for fast recovery. |
| 23. | Snail | *Nula lhinuo* | Raw snail is gulped to cure gastric problems. |
| 24. | Squirrel | *Keli* | Meat is cooked and eaten for cough. It also gives strength and nourishment to the body. |

*Source:* Fieldwork

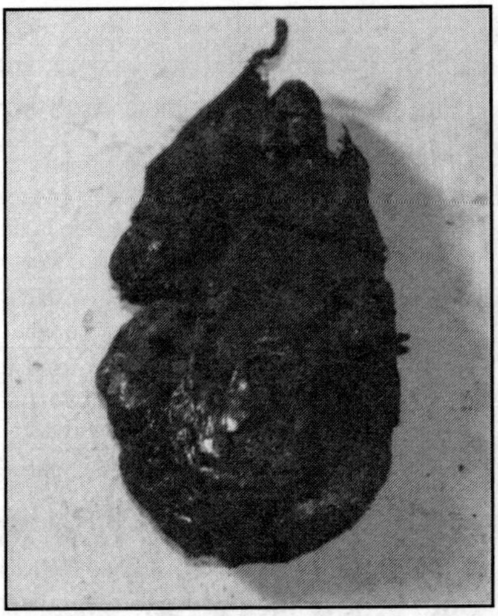

**(1) Dried bile of porcupine**

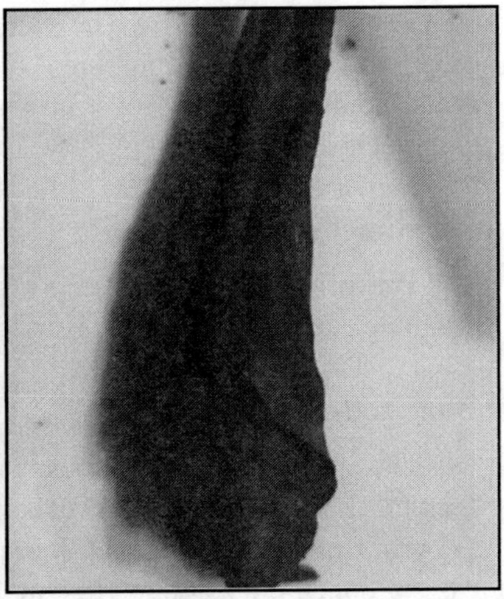

**(2) Dried bile of monkey**

(3) Scale of pangolin

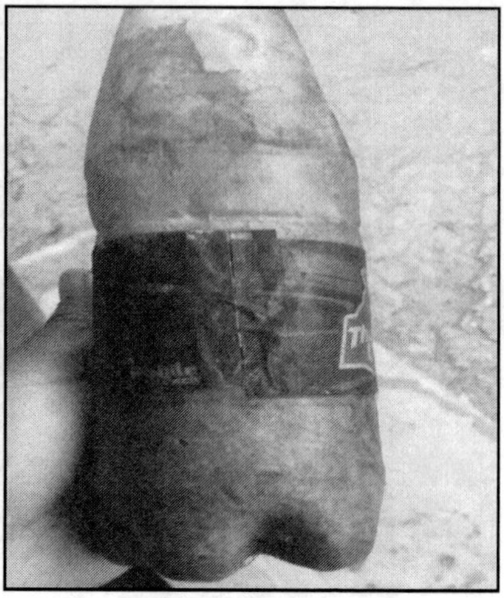

(4) Preserved python fat

*Source:* Fieldwork

Apart from plants and animals, other methods of treatments include the use of charcoal for cleaning teeth, kerosene applied on cuts for blood clotting, and urine (*pezu*) on sore eyes for conjunctivitis. Likewise, even human hair is also tied at the base of a skin tag which usually falls off painlessly on its own after a few days. To bring a boil to the head, a little yeast is rubbed over it. When ripe, it is lanced with a sharp object to drain the pus. For cuts caused by sharp objects like spear or *dao*, the same object should be licked for relief. The same can also be cured by a paste prepared by grinding sugar and applying it on cuts and wounds. Honey (*mepfi dzii*) is also applied on ulcers and is also used as a medicine for gastric problems and hiccups as well.

## Ethnomedical specialist

The different types of healers in the village are identified as bonesetters, fishbone extractors, midwives, and faith healers.

## Bone setters

The word Bone setters in Angami are known as "*u phi u rou chiiya kezamia*". The village have two well-known bonesetters; Vikeduotuo (31 years, male) and Medovi (38 years, male) who provide treatment in the case of bone injury or bone fracture. Both believe their ability to heal is a gift from God and should be used for the welfare of the people. To heal fractured bone or dislocation, they gently massage the affected area with mustard oil (*mithatier*) or with ethnomedical remedy known to them and thereby resets the bone. The treatment is usually performed without any fees however sometimes people offer them chicken or other vegetables out of gratitude.

### Fishbone extractor

A fishbone extractor is a person who can remove fish bones or any other small bones which get stuck in the throat.

Thepfuhie-o (74 years, male) is a well-known fish bone specialist. The story on how he received the gift of removing fish bones in the throat is as follows:

There is a belief that a person who can kill an otter (*khuorha)* by biting it acquires the power to remove fish bones getting stuck in the throat. His father and his grandparents used to tell him the same story. One day he went hunting towards a place called "*va khetsaye*" and on his way back home, he saw an otter coming towards him in the stream. As he saw the otter, he quickly took out his gun and shot and injured the animal. He then hurriedly picked the animal and bit it with his teeth as hard as possible till it was completely dead. It is also believed that a person who kills an otter should not eat its flesh. So he refrained from eating the meat of the otter and thereafter he got the ability to remove bones that get stuck in the throat by gently massaging the neck with his hands and in the process utters:

"A n perhi, n dukhri ketsii mia
A n perhi, n ta khri ketsii mia,
Khoto ro khota moro ke tuo ro ke ta"
"I am your slayer
I injure and bite you alive
Come up if you must or go down"

As he does this, the fishbone automatically disappears from the throat. Alternatively, the palm of the animal can be used to gently rub the throat to remove the bones. After this, the patient is advised to swallow rice without chewing to make sure the bone has slipped down.

### Midwives/Traditional Birth Attendant

Regarding matters relating to pregnancy and delivery of a child, midwives (mostly elderly women) are consulted. Three midwives are identified in the village namely, Neizotuoii (72 years), Monuo (74 years) and Sisieii (75 years) who cater to the needs of the pregnant women. Deliveries take place either at home or in the absence of midwives or in case of complications, hospitals are sought. All midwives advise pregnant women to stay active and refrain from taking bed rest the whole day. In the initial stage of pregnancy, women are to perform her regular normal duties. She is supposed to keep herself busy and active and carry out household chores that ensure easy and quick delivery of a child. Bed rest and idleness are not encouraged by the experts to pregnant women as inactivity results in complications making it more difficult to perform normal delivery.

## Faith healers

Faith healing is a method of treating physical and emotional illness which often involves prayer or laying hands (gestures) believed to elicit divine intervention in healing which is very popular among Christians. It is mostly pastors/ordained ministers who are often sought after for such healing. The faith of the patient in God and faith of the religious elders along with their prayers is believed to be the vital elements to bring healing to the sick person. Bible passages are read for the sick people, followed by a prayer to appeal to God to change a person's physical or mental condition for the better. This form of faith/divine healing is a popular form of healing among Christians in contemporary times.

## Conclusion

It can be inferred from the study that ethnomedicine remains to be a supportive healthcare system for the people of Viphoma Village. The use of plant resources available in their surrounding area coupled with animal derivatives for treating diseases and infirmity has been part and parcel of their culture. Their deep connection with nature, their cultural attachment to traditional medicine and the lack of modern healthcare facilities have made them rely on ethnomedicine for ages. However, the question of survival and continuity of this medical system arises. The wealth of ethnomedicinal knowledge is mostly confined to the older generation and there are no written documents regarding the same posing a challenge for the younger generation to retain the knowledge. Many healers are not able to pass down the knowledge due to a lack of interest among the youngsters today. If this trend continues then there is a possibility that the rich ethnomedical knowledge might be forgotten in the near future. There is an urgent need for proper documentation of indigenous knowledge relating to healthcare practices not only among the Angamis but also among different tribal groups. Most importantly, research in the field of ethnomedicine is felt more than ever so that this traditional knowledge will be preserved for the benefit of the present and the future generations.

## References

Acharya, D. & A. Shrivastava. (2008) *I. ndigenous Herbal Medicines. Tribal Formulations and Traditional Herbal Practices.* Jaipur: Aavishkar Publishers.

Alves, R. & I. Rosa. (2005). Why study the use of animal products in traditional medicine? *Journal of Ethnobiology and Ethnomedicine*, 1(1), 1- 5.

Bhasin, V. (2007). Medical Anthropology: A Review. *Ethnomedicine*, 1(1), 1-20.

Islam, M. (2009). *Medicinal Plants of North East India*. Jaipur: Mittal Publications.

Mukherjee, P.K. (2002). *Quality Control of Herbal Drugs: An Approach to Evaluation of Botanicals*. New Delhi: Business Horizons Publishers.

Mwchahary, D.D. & D.C. Nath. (2015). Deforestation and its Impact on Ethno-Medicinal Practices among Bodo Tribe of Kokrajhar District in Assam, India. *Journal of Environmental Science, Computer Science and Engineering and Technology*, 4(4), 961-979.

Pfoze, N.L. and D.N. Chiezou. (2006) *D. icentra scandens (D. Don)* Walp.3/4. A highly potent ethnomedicinal plant against malaria, high blood pressure and diabetes. *Indian Journal of Traditional Knowledge*, 5(2): 268-70.

# 11

# Thadou Kukis Beliefs and Practices towards Nature

**Lunminthang lhouvum**

**Abstract**

Culture plays a very significant role in human adaptations towards their nature and Traditional knowledge or indigenous knowledge and its transmission shaped the culture and society of a particular community. The Thadou people are one of the numerous Kuki-Chin groups living in northeast India with numerous settlements in Manipur. They have rich treasure knowledge about their natural surroundings which can be seen in their traditional beliefs and cultural practices. This paper tries to explore how the various beliefs and practices of the Thadou of Manipur, aid in the management and maintenance of their natural surroundings. This paper is an exploratory research work based on ethnographic account, vernacular source, and interviewing knowledgeable village elders. The work seeks to project the importance of traditional knowledge of the Thadou people in the management and conservation of their natural surroundings and the recognition of the people as a part of the ecological system.

**Keywords:** Exploratory research; Resource management; Traditional knowledge; Thadou Kukis.

## Introduction

Indigenous communities had developed a symbiotic and biotic relationship with their natural environment and had a diverse attachment to it. Aside from their economic needs, their socio-cultural practices and beliefs system revolves around their natural environment. The Thadou are a Kuki-Chin ethnic group living in northeast India, with numerous settlements in Manipur. They have a wealth of knowledge about their natural surroundings, as evidenced by their traditional beliefs and cultural practices. This paper attempts to investigate how the various beliefs and practices aid in the management and maintenance of their natural surroundings along with the people's recognition as a part of the ecological system. There is, in fact, a deep connection between land use and their beliefs and socio-cultural practices as to the Thadou people the world is the land they lived in. Their traditional ecological knowledge, acquired through long-term experience with their natural environment over generations, shapes their society and culture. As stated in the abstract, the article explores the Thadou Kuki perspective towards their nature and its manifestation in their traditional beliefs and cultural practices, which can be seen as their way of managing their natural environment. For instance, as yet the Thadou village continues to maintain reserved forests and follow certain beliefs and cultural practices with regard to their natural landscape.

## Context and Methodology

The word "Kuki" is purely a conventional one. It is a term used by the Assamese and Bengali-speaking people to refer to the various hill tribes like that of the Rangkhol, Lushai, Thadou, and others. Based on their migration the Kukis are divided into 'Old Kuki' and 'New Kuki' (Grierson: 1967). 'Thadou' are referred to as New Kukis, which appears so often in the records of Cachar and Sylhet, which has been adopted by Dr. Grierson in the "Linguistic Survey of India" (Shakespeare:1912:189). The Thadou are a Kuki-Chin ethnic group living in the area bounded by the Angami of the Naga hill district in the north, Province of Burma in the East, Chin and Lushai hill in the south, and the district of Cachar in the west (Shaw: 1929:1).

Though the practice of traditional ecological knowledge is very old, little research is known on the Thadou people's relationship with their natural environment. Further, how their beliefs system and cultural practices are entrenched in their adaptation to the environment warrant the investigation. The paper thus is an exploratory research work based on careful examination of existing ethnographic accounts, personal interviews with traditional cultural specialists amongst the Thadou as well as available vernacular sources. Since this is exploratory research there is no defined field area.

## Theoretical framework

Indigenous peoples around the world have preserved distinctive understanding rooted in a cultural experience that guides relations among humans in a specific environment. This understanding and relations constitute a system broadly identified as indigenous knowledge or traditional knowledge. Though the terms traditional knowledge and traditional ecological knowledge (TEK) are interchangeably used and the word "traditional" implies that the concepts are of the past and unchangeable and may not be relevant to the contemporary world. But there are several beliefs and practices of the Thadou which can be considered as a result of scientific curiosity about their natural environment. The term traditional ecological knowledge came to widespread use in the 1980s. The earliest studies on traditional ecological knowledge were carried out by Anthropologists as ethnoecology; an approach that focuses on the concept of the ecological relationship held by people or cultures (Inglis, 1993).

Margereth Bruchal (2014:2). define traditional knowledge as a network of knowledge, beliefs, and traditions intended to preserve, communicate, and contextualise relationships with culture and landscape over time. Though one might distinguish "knowledge" as factual data, 'beliefs' as a religious concept, and 'traditions' as a practice, these terms are often used imprecisely and interchangeably to describe indigenous epistemology. Indigenous knowledge is conveyed formally or informally among kin groups and communities through social encounters, oral tradition, ritual practices, and other activities.

Raymond Peirotti (2011) opines traditional knowledge as local base knowledge of individual people which emerged from careful long-term observation of natural phenomena. Peiroti defines traditional ecological knowledge as the "sum of the data and ideas acquired by human groups on its environment resulting from group usage and occupation of a specific region over generations".

Fikrets Berkes (1999:8) "Sacred ecology" is a cumulative body of knowledge, practice, and beliefs, evolved by adaptive processes and handed down through generations by cultural transmission about the relations of a living being (including human) with one another and with their environment. Berkes approaches traditional ecological knowledge as a knowledge-practice-beliefs complex that examines four interrelated levels: empirical knowledge or practical knowledge; paradigmatic knowledge; institutional knowledge; world view (*Ibid:* 1999:18).

Adam Dunstan (2012:1) Indigenous community possesses a belief in the sacredness of the environment. The way in which indigenous communities related to the environment varies and can be seen in their beliefs and practices that may arise from folk tales, traditions, cosmologies, and other interesting factors, in varied and complex ways. To Dunstan, changes in certain aspects of an indigenous community such as language and subsistence (technology) do not affect sacred ecology of a group or community's spiritual relationship with the environment. (*ibid:* 2012:2).

In the backdrop of the above, the study explores the relations between some aspects of ecology or ecological infrastructures like a land pattern of land utilisation, forest, certain agricultural practice, and some aspects of a social institution and practices like chieftainship, ritual and traditional forest management of the Thadou people.

## Sacred Landscape and Beliefs System

The Thadou believed that the whole world including trees, forests, mountains, stones, and rivers was the manifestation of paramount power called '*Pathen*' and was protected by several malevolent spirits who necessitated constant pacification. They believed in a forest god called "*Thingbulnga*" having its jurisdiction in the jungle alongside the river god and god of mountain and rocks. The god of rivers, mountains, and metal have no distinct name then that of the matter over which they provide and are merely called "*tui pathein*" or water god, "*thi pathein*" or iron god (Steward:1885:629). In addition, *Thempu* (priest) plays a very crucial role in the beliefs and cultural practices of the Thadou. Natural landscapes with enormous size and unique structures such as a mountain, rocks, and large trees are held sacred by the people prior to undertaking any activities with it or around it, they have the practice of asking permission verbally before undertaking any activities. A few places which are held sacred by the Thadou people are identified as *Koubru Mol, Kolkang, Karot Kol, Kaineng Kol, Vangai Lhang, Makoi Lhang.*

As far as beliefs with regards to water usage are concerned, the Thadou prefers water that is drawn from streams, rivers, and subterranean aquifers. Though very little care is taken care of the water source from where water is drawn and many people resort to bathing and washing clothes near the water sources. Since bathing proclivities of the Thadou are uncommon, the contamination of water is slight. Further, the water sources that are held sacredly by the people are '*Shi*' (marshes and swamp) and '*Tuisam*' (water spring). These sources of water are revered for the belief that spirits reside in these water bodies. As such, they adhere to do's and don'ts in order to maintain sacredness. For example, they prevent the raising of certain vegetables such as Taro, Chilli, etc nearby these water bodies.

## Rituals and Beliefs Associated with Agricultural Practices

The Thadou are constantly on move, rarely occupying a particular place for more than two years or at the most three years at a time before they move to a new site following exhaustion of the land of essential nutrients. Their mode of cultivation is called '*Kanglei'* (jhum cultivation) starting with a practice known as *'lou munvet', 'lou'* means 'fields', '*munvet*' means selection as per the area earmarked by the chief for jhum cultivation for that particular year. A representative from each household of the village would go to the jungle to mark the site for cultivation; this practice is known as *'Lou Chan'* (Sitlhou, 2020:451). The Thadou people have this particular belief and practice called 'Mang san' and *'Je chan*', a ritual practice to ascertain positive affirmation from the spirit of the land on whether they could cultivate the jhum site for that particular year. Once it is affirmed by the *Thempu,* on an appointed day all villagers go to the site and set the field on fire. Once the field was set on fire it was customary to remain indoors throughout the next day. Further, the tradition of remaining indoors is called '*vam nit*', *vam* means 'ashes' and '*nit*' means 'observance'. This observance is also symbolic of condolence to all the animals and insects that have perished in the jungle fire, to award off the relatives of those animals who were killed in the forest fire and to avoid the wrath of *Gampi Gampu* (the spiritual owner of the jungle) (Lhouvum, 2014).

*'Daiphu'* is a ritual performed by *Thempu* after burning the jhum field and before sowing. The rituals depict a sense of environmentalism and the notion of sacred realms of the Thadou (Shaw: 1929:77). To strengthen the soil fertility furthermore they practice '*Louchul Thoat*' which is a peculiar practice of the Thadou, wherein repetition of jhum cultivation in the same site is restricted and if any individual is found defaulting in the same site, he or she is heavily penalised in kind by sacrificing a pig and seeking of forgiveness to the village chief '*Housa*' and his council "*Semang Pachong*". '*Chang nungah*' is another belief and practice of the Thadou. The ritual is performed so as to receive blessings in abundance at the time of harvest. (Kilong: 2012:29). The Thadou did not task their soil after the first or second crop so the rice and agriculture product raised by the Thadou are much superior to that of the Cachar and the Naga people (Steward: 1885:633). Another meticulous practice that is worth mentioning with regard to jhumming is, in case of the existence of '*shi*' (marsh or swamp) in the field. The *thempu* had to perform '*Teikhuh Thoina*' (a ritual seeking the spirit of '*shi*' to grant permission of cultivating the site for a particular year). Though paddy has been the principal crop raised, alongside they

also grow vegetables such as Taro, Bean, Peas and Maize, etc adjacent to the surrounding of the paddy field. Thus, adding to subsistence livelihood.

## Beliefs and Practices Concerning Plants and Animals

Domestication and hunting of animals have been practiced by the Thadou people since time immemorial. They domesticate animals like Mithun (*sel*), Buffaloes, Pigs, Goat, Dogs, Fowls, etc. They are domesticated in their natural habitat. For instance, Buffaloes are allowed to roam freely in the open space during the daytime and are later gathered again from the hillside or forest by evening. This task is known as "*loichin*". Mithun *(Sel)* is left to roam in the jungle on their own, tamed, and is persuaded to collect salt near the village. Further, Mithun has been highly valued and serves many utilities in Thadou Custom and Traditions. In addition, few wild animals such as '*Sasan*' (Burmese deer) and '*Gulpi*' *or 'Sam*' (Python) are believed to have possessed evil spirits, thus the Thadou people avoid hunting these animals.

Trees occupy a significant place owing to their functional utility among the Thadou people. They used trees for varied purposes such as Timber, Materials for building their houses and as Firewood, etc. As such, there is a preferred time when Trees could be felled following the positioning of the moon. For instance, when the lunar size decreases from full moon to new moon, the period is considered favourable for felling trees because trees felled during this period are thought to be more durable, sturdy and they are not easily rotten. Though the Thadou are fond of fruit trees they also held the concept of forbidden trees i.e. Trees that are not desired to be raised within the house compound. Few such trees in local dialects and the justification why they are forbidden are:

*Mong thing* (the trees has widespread roots covering up large area of the house compound)

*Long lhi* (as the name suggest it resemble human tears)

*Thing hang* (when in contact this tree cause irritation and allergy)

*Mot saiso* (belonging to the banana family; they make an unusual sound while they grow)

## Beliefs and Practices Pertaining Village Settlement

Each and every Thadou village is demarcated by hillocks, streams, rivers, ridge, etc. In the olden days when the Thadou occupied a new land, they seek *'Gampi Gampu*' (spiritual owner of land) who is considered to be the spirit of the virgin land, and rituals known as '*mangsan*' then follow (mangsan is a ritual that involves sacrificing white cock to the spirit of the land and wait to ascertain approval through their dream). At the village level even though the chief held the sole authority and received a basket full of rice called (*changseu*) from the villagers as a form of tax. He has no say with regard to the distribution of land to all individual families for cultivation purposes which take place every year as and when the Jhum field shifts annually.

The Thadou village is surrounded by its reserved forest called "*khotu*" or '*Gamkheh*'. They also make '*meilam*' (literally means fire way) which functions as a buffer zone against turbulent wildfire and the village settlement and this area are preserved for procuring wild fruits, vegetables, and dead woods (Haokip:2006:49). Beyond the reserved forest was a cultivating zone called "lougam" and at the outer circle was the hunting zone. This is the part of the forest where many of the malevolent spirits are believed to reside, also termed sacred groves wherein any harm caused to it increases the likelihood of the wrath of the supernatural spirit upon the whole village community and it was for this reason that the village *thempu* (priest) had to constantly make sacrifices to ensure the safe and successful return of the hunters (Kipgen & Haokip, 2021). Thadou also held the practice of keeping "*Houn*" kitchen garden where different types of locally available vegetables are grown, further adding to their subsistence livelihood.

## Traditional Food Preservation Practices

The tribal economic system of the Thadou and ways of living revolve around ecological parameters like territorial land and forest. It is through their local knowledge system that they are able to obtain their daily food requirement from nature and natural resources are utilised at their best sustainable level without disturbing their ecology. Further, the food preservation practices of the Thadou were identified as a precondition to secure and reliable sources of food even during the off-season and in times of food shortage. For example, Vegetables are preserved in a dried form called '*Anche goup*'. They are kept in appropriate storage facilities '*Gap lheng*' (mantel) which is a form of the traditional preservation method. Another popular means of food preservation is by the process of fermentation knowns as '*Athu or kibil*'. Vegetables such as Soyabean, Bamboo shoot, Meat, and Leafy vegetable are preserved using this method (*Ibid*, p.144) thereby facilitating food availability and continuity during off-season.

## Conclusion

The paper highlights the Thadou Kuki perspective towards their natural environment thereby revealing close proximity and relationship between them. To them, the world is the land they lived in and any harm meted to them will incite the wrath of the supernatural god. The priest '*Thempu*' plays a very big role in Thadou society and acts as the middleman between the people and the supernatural god *Pathen*. This work also examined how the cultural practices and beliefs system of the Thadou reveal scientific curiosity and that their traditional knowledge does not merely compass matters of immediate interest but also help in optimal resource utilisation without disturbing their ecology. Upto the present time, some of the traditional knowledge of Thadou Kuki hold a special space in the life of the Thadou people. Further, the present paper is only a small endeavour to advance the research quest on traditional ecological knowledge of the Thadou Kukis.

## Notes

1. The term ecology was first coined by German Biologist, Ernest Haeckel from two Greek words 'Oikos' meaning 'house or dwelling' and 'logos' meaning 'science or study'.
2. *Mol* means hill or mountain.
3. *Kol* means the steep mountain
4. *Lhang* means base of a mountain
5. *Lhi* means tears.
6. *Gap lheng* is a mental built above the fireplace for drying or storing preserved foods items.
7. *Seman Pachong* means the council of village elders appointed by the chief.
8. *kanglei* means jhum cultivation.
9. *Shi* means marsh or swamp.
10. *Tuisam* means Spring water.
11. Lhouvum kailal, Cultural Specialist from Motbung, Secretary Custom and Culture, Elmun Council, interviewed on 5th October 2021.
12. Thongkholam Lhouvum, Village Authority Member, in charge of the forest, Interviewed on 3rd October 2021.

## References

Berkes, Fikrets. (1999). *Sacred Ecology.* London. Routledge.

Boruchal, Magareth (2014). Indigenous Knowledge and Traditional Knowledge. *Encyclopedia of Global Archeology 3814-3824,* p. 1.

Dunstan, Adan. (2012). What was damaged? Taking Sacred Ecology into Account in Environment Impact Assessment, *Indigenous Policy of Journal.* Vol. XXII, No.4. pp.1-2.

Grierson, G. A. (1967). *Linguistic Survey of India Vol.III. Tibeto-Burman Family. Part III. Specimen of Kuki Chin & Burman Group.* Delhi. Motilal Banarsidas.

Haokip, D. L. (2006). *Traditions and Customary Laws of the Chassad*. Ph.D. A thesis submitted to Department of History. Manipur University, Canchipur.

Inglish, Julian T. (1993). *Traditional ecological: Concept and Cases*. Ottawa. International Program on Traditional Ecological knowledge & International Development Research Centre.

Kilong, Helthang. (2012). *Khul Peng Ho Chonna Khanna*. Motbung. Helthang Kilong.

Kipgen, Ngamjahao & Haokip, D.L. (2021). *Against the empire; Polity, Economy during the Aanglo Kuki War, 1917-1919.* London: Routledge.

Lhouvum, Kailal (2014). *Thadou-Kuki Chondan (Custom) Leh Tamenglong District Kho Leh Veng Ana Mang Ho Thusim.* Motbung. Kailal Lhouvum.

Pierotti, Raymond. (2011). *Indigenous knowledge of Ecology and Evolutionary Biology*. New York. Routledge.

Shakespear. J. (1912). *The Kuki Lushai Clans*. London. Macmilan & Co. Limited.

Shaw, William. (1929). *Notes on the Thadou Kukis*. Government of Assam.

Sithlhou, H. (2020). Sacred Ecology and ritual practices of the Thadou Kukis of Manipur. *The Eastern Anthropologist.* Vol. 73.3-4, p. 451.

Steward, R. (1855). Notes on Northern Cachar. *Journal of Asiatic Society of Bengal.* Vol. XXIV. pp. 628-629.

# 12

# The Indigenous Practices of Korku Tribe of Melghat, Yavatmal

**Abhishek Kumar and Amit Kumar**

**Abstract**

Korku Tribe is one of the poorer and most deprived tribal groups in India, mostly residing in Maharashtra and Madhya Pradesh. The Korku tribe resides in the Melghat region of Maharashtra, which is very famous for its backward development. The lower socio-economic status has impacted them badly as most of these tribes are malnourished, and child mortality cases are very common. The Korku tribes of this region still do not have the proper health-care facilities, due to which their indigenous medicinal practices are very common. This paper will discuss the use of indigenous medicinal practices by the Korku Tribe of Melghat, Yavatmal region.

**Key Words:** Korku, Indigenous medicinal practices, Melghat.

## Introduction

Every tribal community, including the Korku tribe, possesses their traditional knowledge, beliefs and practices relevant to good health. Healthcare in tribal communities is mostly associated with their strong relationship with local and natural resource bases. Their indigenous knowledge of medicines, herbs and rituals is foundational to supporting the community's health for centuries in remote areas of their habitat. Most of the people from the Korku tribes are quite distinct culturally from the mainstream society regarding livelihood, traditions, rituals etc. They are culturally and geographically detached from other groups with diverse backgrounds and histories. From an anthropological perspective, tribal people are indigenous to the soil, inhabit forestry and hilly areas, pursue a subsistence-level economy, practice their traditional religion and culture, and believe in common ancestry (Awasthi, 2021).

Similarly, the Korku tribe is one of the poorer and most deprived tribal communities in India. This tribe predominantly resides in the region of Maharashtra and Madhya Pradesh. In Maharashtra, Melghat in the Yavatmal region has a significantly better share of the population of the Korku tribes. Among the Korku tribe, malnourishment and child mortality is high due to poor healthcare facilities in the region. As a result, they rely on Indigenous Medicinal practices except for the ancestral one. However, only indigenous medicinal practices cannot be relied on for better health in the long run. There is a need to have integrated indigenous and modern healthcare facilities. Therefore, this paper attempts to discuss the use of indigenous medicinal practices by the Korku Tribe of Melghat.

## Research Methodology

The research methodology used for writing this paper is qualitative type. For the study, the data was collected from these villages; *Bori* and *Chitri* from Harishal Gram Panchayat and *Kotha* from Jambu Gram Panchayat. These villages are located in the Melghat, Yavatmal region of Tiger Reserve, dominantly inhabited by the Korku tribe population, who runs. Out of these, 71 families were selected for study as a sample through the household survey method. The data has been compiled from both primary and secondary sources. For Primary sources, data has been collected through various techniques like interview schedules and Case Studies. The respondents in the Interview Schedule include people from the community. For the case study, the medical practitioners were consulted for in-depth knowledge.

Along with this, data has also been collected from secondary sources through research papers, government documents, the internet, books etc. In this research, village sarpanch and elders of the house have been selected for the compilation of family data, as well as traditional doctors, mainly *Jadi Baba*, who acquire knowledge about herbs through their practice.

## About Korku Tribe

### Origin Story

There is no written proof about the origin of Korku, but there is a glimpse of the origin of this tribe based on the cosmic story of a divine origin. Once, Ravana, the famous king of Lanka, came to Vindhyachal and Satpura regions. While walking to the sanctuary, he noticed an unlucky, very quiet place where no one lives. Then, Ravana requested God Mahadev to make this place alive with animals and humans. In response, God

Mahadev became happy and ordered Kagdoot Kageshwar to bring red soil from the Bhanwargarh and Sawligarh. Mahadev made a human-like effigy from the red clay soil and was about to give the breath in that effigy, but at the same time, God Indra got angry because of Mahadev's activities and sent his horse. The horses sent by Indra destroyed the clay-made effigy. Later on, from the same soil, the effigy of a dog was made, who ran after the horses. Then after, Mahadev made the two human-like effigies named 'Mulaa' as Male and 'Mulai' as female, giving them breath to live. Both the Mulaa and Mulai became the founders of the Korku tribe. The place where the Kagdoot Kageshwar brought the soil is Sawligarh and Bhanwargarh. This place is considered to be the origin of the Korku tribe. The Korku tribe usually dig (Korna or Kodna in Hindi) the roots in forests of the Vindhyan and Satpura range which is later called Korku. 'Kor' or 'Koro', which means 'Man' and 'Ku' means "Alive"; thus, Korku means 'Alive Men' (Biswas, 2017).

## Demography Details

As per the 2011 census, the total population of the Korku Tribe in India is 9,55,399. In Maharashtra, their total population is 2,64,492 and the rest are in Madhya Pradesh. The languages spoken by this community are Korku, Marathi and Hindi. The literacy rate of the Korku tribe in Maharashtra is 73.40 percent. Male literacy is higher than female literacy, i.e., 82.39 percent for males and 64.02 percent for females. The Sex ratio in the Korku tribe in the Maharashtra region is 960 per thousand males. The child (0-6 years old) sex ratio is 973 per thousand males (GOI, 2011).

As per the data recorded by the researcher in three villages, the total population (including Korku tribes and others) in Chitri, Kotha and Bori villages are mentioned below in Table 1.

**Table 1: The Demographic Details**

| Details | Chitri | Kotha | Bori |
|---|---|---|---|
| Total Population | 348 | 1064 | 1060 |
| Male Population | 181 | 571 | 553 |
| Female Population | 165 | 493 | 507 |
| Literacy rate | 70.16% | 83.40% | 72.81% |
| Sex ratio | 911 | 863 | 917 |

## Indigenous Medicinal Practices

Indigenous medicinal practices have maintained a special position in many south Asian countries like India, China, Japan, Pakistan etc.

Indigenous Medicinal Practices are part of the health healing practices mostly among the tribal communities as they inhabit the forestry region with considerable knowledge of identifying the flora and its uses. It is the way of defending and restoring the health that has been passed to the present generations from the past generations. The traditional medical practices of the Korku are famous, as the Melghat region is a land of many precious herbs and shrubs. The practice of traditional medicine has been wildly widespread until recently, but the weakening state of traditional medical practice was evident from the field research. Many ward elders reported that they completely depended on traditional medicine for all kinds of physical ailments. The Melghat region is notorious for health matters and the prevalence of various illnesses (E.P., 2020). The Korku tribe in the Melghat region is one the tribes that also rely on traditional medicinal practices for health healing. *Jadi Baba* mainly treats people through herbs, so these people are more knowledgeable about herbs. The details of the various diseases and their treatment with traditional medicinal products are as follows:

## Dysuria (Burning Urination)

Dysuria makes the patient feel pain or a burning sensation during peeing or urination. Males and females of any age group can experience this disease. The Korku people use *Gwarpatha* (Scientific Name: Aloe Vera) for the treatment. They drink one glass of *Gwarpatha* jelly with sugar mixed in it for seven days and recover from the illness. During the medication week, they do not take any meat or fish.

## Foot Pain due to Thorn Prick

This pain happens when part of the pricked thorn got stuck inside the foot sole and started to hurt after some days. They use *Akaw* (Scientific Name: Calotropis Procera) leaf for the treatment. They foment with the help of this leaf that relieves the pain of the patient. The milk of the *Akaw* leaf helps in coming pricked thorns out of the sole.

## Calculus (Pathari)

It is a compaction of minerals formed inside the body parts, especially in the kidney or gallbladder. It causes too much pain. The patient uses *Dudhi* (Euphorbina Hitra) Plant leaf with water and drink for treatment. It gives relief from the pain of Calculus. This time they do not prefer to eat gram.

**Hemorrhoid**

Hemorrhoids, also known as piles, are swollen veins in the patient's anus and lower rectum, similar to varicose veins. It can develop inside the rectum or under the skin around the anus. For the treatment, the patient takes *Laalgooty* (Scientific Name: Sphaeranthsus Indicus), *Safedgooty* (Scientific Name: Filago; Loefl. ex L.), Teuchi (Scientific Name: Mitragyna Speciosa), *Amarbaal* (Scientific Name: Cuscuta Reflexa), Copper bhaji, koilari leaf (Scientific Name: Bauhinia Monamara), Jadkumbhi (Scientific Name: Portulacaoleracea) plants after soaking it in water for 24 hours. Then, filter it in the morning and drink. This medication takes 15 days to get cured.

**Fracture**

The bone fracture can be treated with the help of hair, egg, and the vermilion offered to God Hanuman. All are wrapped in a cloth and tied to the broken place; pouring it from time to time can cure the fracture. *Hadjodi* (Scientific Name: Cissusquadr Angularis) also helps in curing fractures.

**Asthma**

It is a condition in which a patient feels difficulty breathing. For the treatment, the patient consumes a paste mixture made up of *Hasbell,* Torah seeds, Honey and Bhilwa water. Bhilwa water is the water that remains in hollow spaces of the tree after rain and fog. The problem of breathing is reduced after consuming this water.

**Jaundice**

Jaundice makes her face, eyes and nails yellow. For treatment, *Teuchi* (Scientific Name: Mitragyna Speciosa), *Tikari* (Luziola Juss), *Amarbaal* (Scientific Name: Cuscuta Reflexa), Mango bark etc., are soaked in water and drunk as medicine by the patient.

**Dog Bite**

For the treatment of dog bites, *Amarbaal* (Scientific Name: Cuscuta Reflexa) *and White Akaw* (Scientific Name: Calotropis Procera) is made into powder into a tablet. Ten tablets are generally preferred to take for the complete cure. Meat and fish are to be avoided during the medication period.

## Snake Bite

When a person gets bitten by a poisonous snake, they prefer to take *Kadulim* (Scientific Name: Azadirachta Indica) by making a solution with water; the patient is made to palpate.

## Malnutrition

Malnutrition is a crucial problem in the Korku tribes of the Melghat region of Yavatmal. The deficiency of many Vitamins is evident from the bodily structure of the Korku tribe because most children, youths, and adults have stunted growth and other health problems caused by inadequate nutrition. Malnutrition is cured by taking a bath continuously for ten days after mixing elephant dung with *Bhumka root (*Scientific Name: Costus speciosus*)* and water.

## Fever

Seasonal fever is one of the common diseases found in the Melghat region. For treatment, Korku people Grind one spoon of Sagwan (Scientific Name: Tectona Grandis) in the morning and evening to cure fever.

**(Scientific Name Courtesy: Botanical Garden Bori)**

## Conclusion

The accessibility of Health remains a critical challenge for the Korku tribes of Melghat in the Yavatmal district. Traditional medicinal practices have been widely practiced for many physical ailments in this region. The study indicates that such medicinal practices act as an emergency aid due to the lack of modern medical facilities. They would try to meet the *Jadi Baba,* but at the time, it may take longer than expected for the cure. At worst, the patients are left in miserable conditions and eventually die.

However, Korku Tribes take proper care of their health and hygiene with indigenous medicinal practices in their village area. The need of the hour is to have proper connectivity with professional medical practitioners and modern healthcare facilities. The governments should promote Indigenous medicinal practices to increase the efficiency of curing diseases and gain the trust of people who are losing interest in such practices. Ultimately, indigenous knowledge is the root of the Korku community culture, which makes them socially alive till now, so this knowledge must be protected through various interventions with the help of Government Organisations and Non-Government Organisations.

## References

Wasthi, M. M. (2021). Health Practices among Tribes in India. *Ancient Indian Wisdom for Sustainable Wellbeing* (pp. 246-253). Varanasi: Bharati Prakashan.

Biswas, R. K. (2017). Changing educational scenario of a scheduled tribe of Madhya Pradesh. *International Journal of Multidisciplinary Research and Development*, 200-206.

E.P., H. R. (2020). The Korku Tribe of Melghat in India and their current state: An Ethnographic Study. *The Oriental Anthropologist*, 97-112.

GOI. (2011). *Individual Scheduled Tribe Primary Census Abstract Data and its Appendix.* New Delhi: Census of India.

# 13

# Academic learning during the Covid-19 pandemic among the tribal students of higher education in Nagaland

**Dr. Jenny Jami**

**Abstract**

The present study attempts to assess the various modes of academic learning among the tribal students of higher education in Nagaland during the Covid-19 pandemic and examine the perception of the students towards these alternative modes of learning. Data for the study was collected from 100 tribal students pursuing higher education in Nagaland. The study yielded observations on varying modes of online education adopted by higher educational institutions in the state and the responses of students towards such changes.

**Key words**: *Pandemic, online education, e-learning, learning-management systems.*

## Introduction

The Covid-19 disease that was declared as a pandemic by the World Health Organisation in March 2019 (WHO, 2020) has drastically affected countries worldwide since its emergence. At the peak months of its spread and consequent containment, it has brought normal daily activities at a standstill. Every aspect of social and economic life of people was affected, including education. Lockdowns, restrictions and curfews were imposed all over in order to contain the spread of the disease. Education, in such a crisis situation, was also deeply affected as schools, colleges and universities remain closed. In India, all educational institutions were ordered to be closed from March 2020. Initially, education was suspended, however, following that, educational buildings were closed. This affected the millions of students across various ages in India, including those pursuing their higher education. In the wake of such an unprepared crisis, many educational institutions started experimenting and adopting varying modes of emergency remote education, particularly online education. Such drastic change in the mode of education from traditional to online education is not without its pros and cons. As online education or e-learning (Aggarwal, 2009; Gaikwad & Randhir, 2015) is adopted by almost all educational systems all over the world and even in India, it has become increasingly important to understand about the same, particularly in the context of rural and tribal populations. Since the country struggles with the issues of a vast digital divide, much remains to be explored in terms of the application, usage, utility and impact of e-learning among the students. The present study, thus, attempts to explore in this direction with an objective to assess the various modes of academic learning among the tribal students of higher education in Nagaland during the Covid-19 pandemic and examine the perception of the students towards these alternative modes of learning.

**Higher Education in Nagaland:** An understanding of the higher education scenario in Nagaland is necessary to develop a contextual background for the present study which is, hence, being discussed in this section. Formal education in Nagaland can be traced to colonial roots and dates back to 1895 when the first school, Clark Memorial Higher Secondary School (CMHSS) was established in the Naga Hills by American Baptist Missionaries (Khuvung, 2008; Oldest educational institute, 2020). Prior to the advent and spread of formal education, the Nagas had a traditional system of youth dormitories, commonly referred to as the *Morung* which served as an institution of learning, educating and imparting traditions, customs, skills, etc. to the young people (Kahmei, 2021; Phom & Zeliang, 2020). With the socio-cultural, economic and political changes over time and the spread of modern education, the *Morung* system slowly declined and was gradually replaced by modern formal educational institutions such as schools, colleges and universities. The focus on education in the country gained momentum after independence, although in Nagaland, formal higher education started quite late in 1959 with the establishment of Fazl Ali College in Mokokchung. Initially, the responsibility for evolving general policy of Higher Education in the State was vested with the Department of Education from which a separate department, Department of Higher and Technical Education under the state government had been established on 1st May 1983 and since then, this department has been given the mandate for formulating and administering the higher education policies in the state. At present, as per the updated reports for the year 2020-2021, there are

66 colleges in Nagaland, which includes 15 government colleges and 51 private colleges. Of these 66 colleges, 21 are located in the district of Kohima, 26 in Dimapur, six in Mokokchung, three in Tuensang, two each in Wokha, Peren, and Phek, and one college in Zunheboto, Kiphire, Longleng and Mon districts. The total number of degree students enrolled in the colleges is 31,311, with 23,017 students enrolled in private colleges and 8,294 students in government colleges. With regards to universities, the state has one Central University i.e. Nagaland University, and three Private Universities namely, St. Joseph University, Dimapur; The Global Open University Nagaland, Dimapur; and the Institute of Chartered Financial Analyst of India University, Dimapur. Most of the colleges are affiliated to Nagaland University with only three Autonomous Colleges and one Institute of National Importance (Department of Higher Education, n.d.).

**Objective of the Study:** The objective of the present study is to assess the various modes of academic learning among the tribal students of higher education in Nagaland during the Covid-19 pandemic and examine the perception of the students towards these alternative modes of learning.

## Methodology

***Study Population:*** For the present study, data was collected from the students of higher educational institutions in Nagaland. Respondents were selected through purposive sampling techniques where an attempt was made to include students from higher educational institutions (HEIs) who were willing to cooperate in the study. A total of 100 students (40 male and 60 female students) pursuing their higher education from various colleges, institutes and universities in Nagaland participated in the study. Data for the present study was collected during September 2021 to December 2021.

***Methods of Data Collection****:* The entire data was collected using structured questionnaires prepared in Google forms and circulated through instant messaging platforms like emails, WhatsApp and Telegram. Information on various aspects of academic learning in higher education during the Covid-19 pandemic was collected through the questionnaire.

***Statistical Analysis of Data****:* Descriptive statistical analysis of data was done using frequency and percentage analysis. Data entry and analysis was done using Microsoft Excel and SPSS (Statistical Package for Social Sciences) software.

## Results and Discussion

***Characteristics of the respondents:*** The present study was conducted among students of higher education in Nagaland. A total of 100 students participated in the study. The basic characteristics of the respondents are shown in Table 1. The ages of the respondents range from 19 years to 25 years. The mean age of the respondents was 21.33 years. The respondents included 40 male students and 60 female students. Most of the respondents were degree level students (80%) while there were also some post graduate level students (17%) and few students of professional courses (3%). Majority of the participating students were from private colleges/ institutes/ universities (63%) while the rest of the respondents were from government colleges/ institutes/ universities (37%). For the present study, the students' responses were received from across 15 private and nine government HEIs in the state. Most of the participating students (75%) were pursuing their higher studies from the colleges/ institutes/ universities located at Kohima, the state's capital. With regard to the residence of the respondents, it was observed that the majority of the students (81%) were residing at home during the Covid-19 pandemic, while a few were staying at rented rooms/ apartments (14%) and paying guest rooms/ hostels (5%). Most of the students were staying at residences located in urban settings (83%) while some of the students were staying at residences located in semi-urban (3%) or rural settings (14%).

***Academic learning during the Covid-19 pandemic:*** The medium and methods adopted for academic learning during the Covid-19 pandemic is presented in Table 2. In this regard, information was collected for the academic semester that was in session during the duration of the study which was from September 2021 to December 2021. It is observed that while most of the higher educational institutes still conduct their classes in online mode (59%), however, with the relaxation in the Covid-19 lockdown regulations, many colleges have started to conduct classes through blended mode (41%). In either case, academic education included a continued focus on online teaching and learning. For the online classes, teachers were found to use either a single medium of e-learning or a combination of two or more applications. It is observed that the most common single medium or application utilised by teachers for conducting online classes was Google classroom (29%). A few of the teachers were found to utilise their respective college mobile applications/ college portals only (9%) which also suggest that some of the colleges have developed and are using their own electronic learning management systems (LMS). It is also seen that few teachers have relied solely on popular messaging applications like WhatsApp/ Telegram as a medium for conducting their classes (6%). Though the use of a single medium for e-learning is common, however, there are many teachers who have used multiple mediums for conducting classes. The most common combination is that of WhatsApp/ Telegram & Google Classroom (34%), followed by WhatsApp/ Telegram & College LMS (4%), Google Classroom and College LMS (3%). About 15 percent of the educators are seen to have utilised all of these applications for conduct of their classes. With regard to the teaching-learning methods during online classes, it was observed that teachers employ either only a single online teaching-learning method or a combination of two or more methods. The most common single online teaching-learning method adopted by teachers was live lectures (40%), followed by upload of self-prepared educational resources such as pre-recorded voice/ video lectures and study notes (8%) or upload of educational resources from other sources (4%). It is also observed that many educators utilised two or more online teaching-learning methods (48%). These include combinations of live lectures and upload of self-prepared educational resources (18%), live lectures and upload of study materials from other sources (5%), upload of educational resources, both self-prepared and those from other sources (5%), and some utilised all of the above teaching-learning methods (20%). For the live lectures/ classes, Google meet was the most common conferencing application used by the teachers (62%), followed by Zoom (8%) and others such as Cisco-Webex (6%). A combination of both Zoom and Google Meet were also used for the conduct of live classes (24%). With regard to the frequency of the online classes, it was observed that classes were conducted regularly for most of the students (44%) or at least four to five times a week (31%) or two to three times a week (17%). However, a few cases of anomaly in the conduct of online classes were also observed with classes being conducted once a week (1%) or rarely (7%).

***Students' self-perception on online academic learning:*** Academic education during the Covid-19 pandemic has undergone a drastic change with the adoption of new methods of online teaching and learning as have already been discussed above. These changes are directly linked with the students, who are the biggest stakeholders in the teaching-learning process. Their opinions and responses to such changes are of immense importance and accordingly, students' opinions/ perceptions on various aspects of online academic learning are also assessed and presented in this study (Table 3). With regard to the students' preferred mode of online teaching-learning, it is observed that majority of students prefer live lectures (60%), followed by upload of self-prepared educational resources by respective teachers (33%) while only a few students preferred upload of relevant study materials from other sources by respective teachers (7%). With regard to the quality of the live classes, most of the students had a positive response with students rating the quality of their live classes as good (44%), average (32%), very good (11%), or excellent (3%). While there was no student in the present study who rated the quality of live classes as very poor, however, there were few students who rated the live classes as poor (10%). The level of students' satisfaction with the conduct of online classes by the teachers was also assessed. Interestingly, it was observed that most students rated their level of satisfaction with the online classes conducted by their teachers as neutral (53%) or satisfied (29%). While it is highly possible that students opted for a neutral stance as they considered their classes as neither good nor bad, however, reasons such as students' hesitancy to rate the quality of the classes conducted by their teachers or their unfamiliarity with the recent mode of online education as a whole cannot be overruled. With regard to the level of students' satisfaction with the initiatives taken by their respective institution/ college/ university for online education, it was found that most of the students were either neutral (48%) or satisfied (41%) with the initiatives taken by their respective institution/ college/ university for online education, though there were few students who were dissatisfied (6%) or very dissatisfied (1%). With regard to the statement on whether online learning is very useful during Covid-19 pandemic, it is observed that majority of the students either agree (40%) or are neutral (35%) with the statement while there are some students who disagree (17%) or strongly disagree (5%) with the statement that online learning is very useful during the pandemic. With regard to the statement on whether online learning can replace the standard classroom education, majority of the students either disagree (40%) or strongly disagree (28%) with the statement while some students had a neutral opinion (21%) and only a few students were found to agree (9%) or strongly agree (2%) with the statement that online learning can replace the standard classroom education.

In addition to the above responses, students' feedback on the advantages, drawbacks and suggestions for improvement of online academic learning was also sought in the present study (Table 4). Based on the feedback provided by the students, it was seen that the biggest advantage of online learning for majority of the students was attending classes from home/ location of their convenience and the associated benefits such as spending more time with family, saving time and money and being able to pursue other hobbies as a result of staying at home (45%). The biggest advantages of online mode of learning for others include self-paced study/ learning (16%), learning and developing new skills (13%), ease of passing exams (3%), better explanation from teachers (2%), and that it was helpful to control the spread of the pandemic (5%). While the online mode of learning was found to be advantageous in many ways, it was disheartening to find that there were also students who did not find online learning advantageous in any respect (11%). Alternatively, when asked about the biggest drawback of online mode of learning, many of the students responded that they tend to easily get distracted or bored/ lose interest of focus (23%). Other drawbacks include poor network connectivity (18%), tendency to become lazy (16%), quality of education being compromised (12%), lesser degree of accountability in attending classes (8%), lesser personal interaction between teachers and students (7%), difficulty in adapting and learning how to use various online learning platforms/ mobile applications (2%), and lack of accountability during exams (2%). Few students even had an extreme opinion that online academic learning is disadvantageous for the students in all respects (5%). Finally, when students were asked about their suggestions for teachers to improve online academic learning, most of them responded that teachers can conduct proper live classes (29%), adopt innovative teaching methods (28%), provide reading materials (9%), show more empathy (9%), and improve internet services (7%). Few of the students responded that the conduct of online academic learning by their teachers was okay and they were satisfied with it (8%) while few responded that they were not sure or had no comment on it (6%).

**Availability and access of electronic and digital resources:** Academic learning through online mode requires availability and access of both electronic and digital resources, and hence, some details on this aspect are included in the present study as shown in Table 5. It was observed that access to internet services were solely through cellular service providers for all the students. Among students using single sim-cards, the popular service providers are Jio (38%), Airtel (26%), and Vodafone (12%). For double sim-card users, the most common combination was that of Airtel and Jio (14%), followed by Vodafone and Jio (5%), Airtel and Vodafone (2%), Vodafone and BSNL (1%) and Jio and BSNL (1%). Many students rated the quality of their internet service as either good (36%) or acceptable (33%), however, there were also students who rated the quality of their internet service as poor (19%) or very poor (4%). Only few students rated the quality of their internet service as excellent (1%) or very good (7%), which is interesting because most of these students were staying at residences located in urban settings where internet services presumably need to be more than acceptable or good. Again, with regard to the ownership and possession of electronic devices to access online education, it was found that most of the students possess only one electronic device for their online learning i.e. smartphones only (73%). Some students were found to possess both smartphones and laptops (21%) while a few of them had smartphones and desktop computers (5%). Only a single student had multiple electronic devices that include smartphone, tablet, laptop and desktop computer. When asked about their acquaintance or familiarity in using electronic devices, most of the students responded that they were good (56%) or average (30%). Regarding whether they sought assistance from others with their online teaching and learning process, it was observed that most of the students sought assistance with their online academic learning (67%) while some students did not seek any additional assistance with their online teaching-learning process (33%). Out of the students who sought assistance, it was observed that students seek help either from a single source or from multiple sources. The most common single source of assistance was classmate-friends (17%), followed by family members (9%) and teachers (7%). Students also sought assistance from multiple sources such as teachers and classmate-friends (12%), classmate-friends and family members (6%), or teachers and family members (2%), while there were few students who sought assistance from all the cited sources (14%). The above discussions, thus, point that the requirements of students for easy access to online learning are to a certain extent inadequate in terms of availability, access and possession of electronic and digital resources and also their training and assistance.

## Conclusion

Online learning or e-learning is not a new concept or approach in academic education. E-learning was introduced and has been functioning as a fundamental part of the student learning experience in higher education over more than two decades and with the Covid-19 pandemic crisis, it has gained much impetus worldwide leading to an unprecedented growth in its application across various educational institutions (Downes, 2005; Ellis et al., 2009). This emphasis on online mode of education has been observed even in the present study where online academic learning was delivered to students through applications such as Google classroom, WhatsApp, and Telegram and in some cases, their respective College LMS/ portals. In the conduct of their online classes, teachers employed either a single online teaching-learning method or a combination of two or more methods. The most common single online teaching-learning method adopted by teachers was live lectures conducted through Zoom or Google Meet, followed by upload of self-prepared educational resources such as pre-recorded voice/ video lectures and study notes or upload of educational resources from other sources. Many educators utilised two or more online teaching-learning methods.

Among the various modes of academic learning that was identified it is observed that the majority of students prefer live lectures and upload of educational resources. Most of the students rated the quality of their live classes as good or average. Most students also rated their level of satisfaction with the online classes by the teachers as well as the initiatives for online education taken by their respective institution/ college/ university as neutral. Majority of the students either agree or are neutral with the statement that online learning is very useful during Covid-19 pandemic. Likewise, most students either disagree or strongly disagree with the statement that online learning can replace the standard classroom education. Such self-reported perception of students may indicate that while online learning has gained acceptance among students, however, traditional mode of classroom learning is rather preferred by the students in general.

The feedback of the students with regard to advantages, drawbacks and suggestions for improvement reveal that flexibility in attending classes from home and its associated benefits was one of the biggest advantages while the biggest drawback for most students was their tendency to easily get distracted or bored. Common suggestions for improvement of online academic learning include conduct of proper live classes by teachers and adoption of more innovative teaching methods. Studies show that student's perception to online learning plays an important role in its effectiveness where it is seen that students who had negative perceptions of the quality of teaching, design, interactivity and workload tended to approach their studies in the course in a comparatively poor way and tended to achieve relatively poorly online; and thus, to improve the quality of the student experience online, addressing student perceptions about what the e-learning experience involves and how it can be useful for learning is essential (Ellis et al., 2009; Mehra & Omidian, 2011).

As online learning gains importance, it also has to be noted that practical problems with regard to utilising these techniques in educational learning environments can be a hindrance to eLearning as has often been observed (Volery, 2000). O'Connell (2002) proposes that students from non-technical backgrounds or those who are more accustomed to traditional face-to-face learning environments, experience problems absorbing course material in eLearning environments. The observation from the present study where students either disagree or strongly disagree with the statement that online learning can replace the traditional face-to-face classroom learning environment reiterates this point. Studies also suggest that a lack of IT skills is considered as one of the main reasons for student non-participation in eLearning courses (Wilson, 2001) and, thus, even undergraduate students should be given focused training on e-learning and on developing their IT Skills in order for them to experience the full benefits of the e-Learning environment (Holley, 2002). While the findings from the present study suggest that students were acquainted with the use of electronic devices, however, it also shows that the majority of them require assistance from others with their online teaching-learning process, and hence, training in these aspects would be highly beneficial for the students. Inability to access technology also cannot be overruled, especially among students with poor economic support. The lack in availability and access of electronic and digital resources can also be found in the present study where all the students are able to access internet services only from one source, viz-à-viz, their cellular service providers and most of them only rely on one electronic device for their online academic learning, viz-à-viz, their smartphones. The present study as well as similar studies have shown (Chitra & Raj, 2018, Ellis et al., 2009; Jardani, 2020; Holley 2002; Mehra & Omidian, 2011; Wilson, 2001) that several factors need to be considered when planning for online or e-learning which includes learners' motivation, learners' attitude towards e-learning, accessibility to technology, technological skills of both learners and educators and availability and access to electronic and digital resources etc. In the case of the higher education students in Nagaland, such factors need to be more critically examined, keeping in mind that learning among the Naga youth has only recently transitioned from traditional *morung* system to modern education and that higher education in the state is still in a young evolving phase.

## References


- Aggarwal, D. (2009, February). Role of e-learning in a developing country like India. In *3rd National Conference, Computing For Nation Development, February* (pp. 26-27).
- Chitra, A. P., & Raj, M. A. (2018). E-learning. *Journal of Applied and Advanced Research, 3*(1), 11-13.
- Department of Higher Education. (n.d.). *Higher Education at a glance*. Retrieved January 1, 2023, from https://highereducation.nagaland.gov.in/higher-education-at-a-glance/
- Downes, S. (2005). E-learning 2.0. *ELearn, 2005*(10), 1.
- Ellis, R. A., Ginns, P., & Piggott, L. (2009). E-learning in higher education: some key aspects and their relationship to approaches to study. *Higher Education Research & Development, 28*(3), 303-318.

- Gaikwad, A., & Randhir, V. S. (2015). E-Learning in India: Wheel of Change. *International Journal of e-Education, e-Business, e-Management and e-Learning, 6* (1), 40-45.
- Holley, D. (2002). "Which room is the virtual seminar in please?". *Education and Training, 44*(3), pp. 112-121.
- Jardani, K. S. A. (2020). E-Learning in Higher Education; Challenges and Opportunities. *International Journal of Innovation, Creativity and Change, 14* (11).
- Kahmei, R. (2021). Morung; Nagas Traditional Education and Centre of Arts and Warfare. *International Journal of Creative Research Thoughts, 9*(4): 570-573.
- Khuvung, L.P. (2008, June 6). CMHSS Impur : the oldest school in Nagaland. *The India Post. https://www.theindiapost.com/*
- Mehra, V., & Omidian, F. (2011). Examining Students' Attitudes Towards E-learning: A Case from India. *Malaysian Journal of Educational Technology, 11*(2), 13-18.
- O'Connell, B. (2002). A poor grade for e-Learning. *Workforce, 81*(7), 15.
- Oldest educational institute in Nagaland turns 125. (2020, November 7). *Morung Express News*. https://morungexpress.com/
- Phom, V., & Zeliang, L. (2020). A Study on the Indigenous and Modern education system among the Phom Tribe in Nagaland. *International Journal of Multidisciplinary Educational Research, 10*(2): 109-111.
- Volery, T. (2000). Critical success factors in online education. *The International Journal of Educational Management, 14*(5), pp. 216-223.
- Wilson, J. (2001). Lessons of a Virtual Timetable: Education. *The Economist*, (17 February), p. 1 (CDROM).
- World Health Organisation. (2020). WHO Director-General's opening remarks at the media briefing on COVID-19 - 11 March 2020.

# Index

## C

## H



## I

## M



## N

## O

## P



## R

## U



## V



## W

**Y**



**Z**